Praise for

little pieces of hope

"Todd Doughty is one of the happiest people on the planet. He finds things big and small that make us smile, and in this wonderful book he shares them with a world he cherishes."

—John Grisham, #1 *New York Times* bestselling author

"Todd Doughty is always the center of the Fun. He gives us nothing less than a party on paper!"

—Chuck Palahniuk, #1 *New York Times* bestselling author of *Fight Club*

"A dazzling spiritual grab 'n' go of big ideas, positive thoughts, and helpful suggestions that will lift and delight readers everywhere. Through the lens of debut author Todd Doughty, the weary world goes Technicolor. Feast on high-octane mixtapes, curated book titles, travel for the curious, and the best in film, theater, and sports. A small-town boy turned big-city seeker, Doughty's personal stories sprinkled throughout pack a wallop as they celebrate family ties, friendship, love, and grief. Josie Portillo's illustrations are glorious. I loved it."

—Adriana Trigiani, bestselling author of *Don't Sing at the Table* and *The Shoemaker's Wife*

"Throughout 2020, Todd Doughty was my Comforter-in-Chief on Instagram. Day after day, he offered his followers poignant, cultural touchstones and Proustian madeleines that ranged from great movies to great books to the small, daily moments when we touch the numinous. He reminded us of the remarkable, exquisite beauty that exists in even the toughest of times, and gave us all reasons to—and here is the greatest gift of all—hope. This book will make you nod with recognition and smile with uncontrollable joy. Bonus? You will also find dozens of new songs and photos and books and musicals and TV series to savor. Everything about *Little Pieces of Hope* is a gem. You will cherish it when the world is smiling upon you and reach for it when the world is closing in."

—Chris Bohjalian, #1 bestselling author of *The Flight Attendant* and *Hour of the Witch*

"Todd Doughty gives us permission to have pleasure. *Little Pieces of Hope* is part meditation / part celebration, a running thank-you note, a time machine that swings us from the Day-Glo eighties to a soft-focus future, a to-do list that guarantees you'll never be bored, a mixtape from a person you want to be your very best friend, a rabbit hole to Wonderland—and we are all Alice. Part recovery / part discovery, this book is a gift for friends, family, and, most especially, yourself."

—Helen Ellis, author of *Bring Your Baggage and Don't Pack Light*

"Todd Doughty has given us the gift of his delight, which is one of the most precious gifts we can collectively receive right now. This lovely collection gives weight to the ordinary and gives levity to heaviness—a cozy antidote to the accumulation of worry. Next time you're tempted to doom scroll, pick up this treasure trove instead: spend time with it and feel your spirit restored and your outlook illuminated. Go out in the world with more ease, and begin to cherish life's joys as Doughty does."

—Mari Andrew, *New York Times* bestselling author of *Am I There Yet?* and *My Inner Sky*

PENGUIN LIFE

little pieces of hope

Todd Doughty is currently senior vice president and deputy publisher at Doubleday and has worked at Penguin Random House for more than two decades. A graduate of Southern Illinois University–Carbondale and former bookseller, he lives with his partner in Westchester County, New York.

little pieces of hope

Happy-Making Things
in a Difficult World

Todd Doughty

ILLUSTRATIONS BY

Josie Portillo

life

PENGUIN BOOKS

An imprint of Penguin Random House LLC
penguinrandomhouse.com

A Penguin Life Book

LIBRARY OF CONGRESS CATALOGING-IN-PUBLICATION
Names: Doughty, Todd, author. | Portillo, Josie, illustrator.
Title: Little pieces of hope: happy-making things in a difficult world /
Todd Doughty; illustrations by Josie Portillo.
Description: [New York, New York]: Penguin Life [2021]
Identifiers: LCCN 2021003521 (print) | LCCN 2021003522 (ebook) |
ISBN 9780143136569 (paperback) | ISBN 9780525508069 (ebook)
Subjects: LCSH: Joy—Miscellanea. | Happiness—Miscellanea. |
Conduct of life—Miscellanea.
Classification: LCC BJ1481 .D68 2021 (print) | LCC BJ1481 (ebook) |
DDC 152.4/2—dc23
LC record available at https://lccn.loc.gov/2021003521
LC ebook record available at https://lccn.loc.gov/202100352

Printed in the United States of America
1st Printing

Set in Horley Old Style MT
Designed by Sabrina Bowers

For my mom,
Linda Sue Church

For her parents,
Walter and Vivian Vaughn
(11/19/1912–5/30/1960 and
6/11/1923–5/30/1960)

For her grandmother,
Rena White (8/31/1889–5/30/1960)

✳ *and* ✳

For Randy Losapio
(the Patrick to my David since 9/6/1996)

and his mom,
Dolores Losapio

little pieces of hope

How This All Came About

On Wednesday, March 11, 2020, on the train home from work, I decided to make on Instagram a little list of "happy-making things in a difficult world," accompanied by a photo I love, as a reminder of the good things that surround us. I thought that others might enjoy it as well, and it'd give them a little piece of hope.

The post was the first of what would become a series on my Instagram (@toddadoughty). It also happened to be the day that the WHO declared a global pandemic.

In the following weeks, as I continued to post lists, I discovered that everyday things mattered more than ever before. Feeling connected mattered more than ever before. And hope mattered more than ever before.

For the past year (up through the moment you're reading this book, in fact), I've kept going. Each day (or so), I curate a random, zigzag, scattershot, hodgepodge selection of stuff that brings joy: everything ranging from short naps to a small piece of chocolate that leaves you wanting more to an extremely green grasshopper to Caillebotte's *Paris Street; Rainy Day* to (my personal favorite, as you will see) Lin-Manuel Miranda. You'll find some of those lists, as well as new ones, in the pages that follow. Additionally, I've made you a few mixtapes, included some "Things You Might Consider Doing Today," and written a few longer essays on particular topics as well (everything from taking the leap to living like *It's a Wonderful Life's* Mary Bailey).

A friend of mine says there is a fine line between memory and discovery. I think she's right. While some items here may be familiar to you, others may not be. My lists should be looked at as a launching pad for you: go forth and forage! If you enjoy something listed here that was previously unknown to you, then we have shared that moment. Conversely, you may not like something on the list, and that's okay too. We all bring different backgrounds and history to the table. My hope is that this book will inspire you to remember and explore the things that bring you happiness, even if they're different from mine (and feel free to cross out things and add your own, so that this book truly becomes yours!).

Whether it's this particular moment in modern history or a regular old bad morning, navigating the day—let alone the hour—can be overwhelming. But we all have touchstones in our lives that we come back to for joy; family, friends, jobs, objects, memories, and experiences are the ties that bind.

My hope is that you look at each list (chronologically or randomly—you do you) and find something that speaks to you, or sparks a memory, or conjures a feeling of happiness and hope. The specificity of the items is key to the experience, such as: *That feeling when you wake up on the first day of vacation; Signing each individual library card with your full name when you checked out a stack of books as a child;* or *Looking back at old diaries or journals and thinking, "Who was that person?"* There's a rhythm and interconnection to each list, which I've carefully crafted for you (and me). The goal was to provide a thought-provoking break in a busy day and a scary world. May this book inspire you to listen, read, watch, look at, spring into action, research, or remember.

Another friend once said to me, "Everybody is carrying an invisible bag of rocks." It's true—I have mine, and you have yours. Each bag may be unique, but the experience is shared. However, I try to look at this in a different light: What's the one (or more) thing, person, book, movie, photograph, painting, recipe, piece of music, or meaningful object that got you through? There are thousands of happy-making things like this in *Little Pieces of Hope.* If this book helped to lighten your burden for even just a minute, then we have shared a moment of hope and joy. In the immortal words of Lillian in the movie *Bridesmaids,* "It's happening." Circle complete.

Happy-making things in a difficult world:

NYC. Fat goldfish. A really good burger. Long walks. Your foot sticking out from under a blanket in order to find some cool air. The music intro to NPR's *All Things Considered*. Short naps. Times Square late at night in the rain. Sondheim. Someone forgiving you. **Someone believing in you.** A really bad DJ at a wedding turning into a really good DJ at a wedding. Stephen King's Twitter. *Twin Peaks* (season 1 still holds up). College basketball. An unexpected phone call or text from someone you haven't talked to in a while but just thought of moments before. An old, gray-muzzled dog with happy eyes. Any movie of Katharine Hepburn's, especially her entrance in *The Lion in Winter*. **A small piece of chocolate** that leaves you wanting more. Ella Fitzgerald's version of Irving Berlin's "Blue Skies." **A long road trip** on a crisp fall day when the leaves are just post-peak and there is a scent of wood smoke in the air. An extremely green grasshopper. **Lin-Manuel Miranda.** The whistle of a train. Katherine Johnson. Newly sharpened pencils. Civility. Bacon. Eudora Welty's *One Writer's Beginnings*. Freshly cut yellow tulips. Caillebotte's *Paris Street; Rainy Day*. The trip home. E. L. Konigsburg's *From the Mixed-Up Files of Mrs. Basil E. Frankweiler*.

Let's keep it going. More happy-making things in a difficult world: The pop of a log in a roaring fire. John Grisham's novel *A Painted House*. A childhood toy or book that you still have. **Any song of Loretta Lynn's** but particularly the bouncy rhythm of "Out of My Head and Back in My Bed" (if you've never heard it, you're welcome). That moment in summer when the light changes its slant and you know fall is on the way. Carrot cake. Those big, fat bumblebees that look like felt toys. The feeling of accomplishment after folding a load of laundry. Ice cream headaches. The pioneering work of Jane Goodall, Dian Fossey, and Biruté Galdikas. **Handwritten thank-you notes.** Marching bands performing pop songs. **Embracing the unexpected.** Walking on a beach with your pants rolled up. Letting it go. Bear hugs. A good haircut. The poems of Shel Silverstein. A walkabout in an empty museum. Picking up with someone you haven't seen in ages and feeling like it was yesterday. Aretha Franklin's recording of "Nessun Dorma." Holiday episodes of your favorite sitcom. Homecoming. A slow dance on a warm night. Blooming dogwoods. Old card catalogs. Lady Bird Johnson. The slap of a high five. The verbal shorthand you have with your college roommates twenty-five years later. Zion National Park. The Eudora Welty House. White, falling-apart peonies.

Happy-making things in a difficult world:

The fact that Anna Wintour went to the movie premiere of *The Devil Wears Prada* wearing Prada. Pitch-black rotary phones. Jeter. Jordan. LuPone. Navratilova. **Three-day weekends** that you forget are three-day weekends when the alarm goes off on Monday morning. Doc Martens. Raindrops on roses and whiskers on kittens ("My Favorite Things" gets a lot of holiday airplay; however, it's not a Christmas song but has lovely lyrics nonetheless). **A really comfy heather-gray hoodie** whose strings you can tug on absentmindedly. Renting a ridiculous rental car. Having an umbrella just when you need it. Having a bookseller recommend a book to you that you needed but didn't know that you needed until you finished it in awe. Jessica Lange in pretty much everything she's ever done but especially *Tootsie*. Brooklyn Duo's instrumental version of a-ha's "Take on Me" (find it on YouTube). **A latte with a design in the foam.** A flight that lands early. Anyone who says, "Love you too." That scene in *Pretty Woman* where Richard Gere slams the jewelry box lid on Julia Roberts's hand and she laughs riotously. A freshly mowed lawn. Mozart's "Requiem." "The Dancing House" (aka the Fred and Ginger building) in Prague. Gershwin's "Rhapsody in Blue" with André Previn playing piano. Those early-December days when it starts getting dark at 4:30 p.m. and you sort of hate it but sort of feel cozy.

Someone saying, **"We're good."**

Someone saying, **"You gave it your best."**

Someone saying, "It's okay."

Putt-putt golf in a seaside town on a blisteringly hot August night.

The dignity of Jacqueline Kennedy Onassis.

Amsterdam.

A cardinal in the wild on a brutally cold winter morning.

Congressman John Lewis.

The act of shelling a pistachio.

Making something new.

E. B. White's *Charlotte's Web*. His stepson, Roger Angell, writing about baseball.

Crossing off the final item on that list of yours.

Oreo Blizzards at Dairy Queen.

Staying up late and hearing **"Live from New York, it's Saturday Night!"**

Keeping calm and carrying on.

Happy-making things **in a difficult world:**

Making friends with strangers while waiting in a long line. Dolly Parton in general, but specifically her bluegrass version of "I Get a Kick Out of You." A very small bouquet of lilies-of-the-valley. The grace of Simone Biles. **Your favorite old T-shirt.** Le Creuset. The Meryl Streep parts of *Julie & Julia*. A really good mixtape (or playlist, for you young ones) made for you by someone else. Vintage photos of 1940s NYC. Driving north on **the Pacific Coast Highway on a cloudless day** when the view is astounding. The smell of a cut lemon. The entire score of *Guys and Dolls*. That day when you realize you're finally over someone who dumped you. Grandmothers. Plaid shirts on a crisp fall day. Red velvet cake. Adriana Trigiani's novel *Lucia, Lucia*. Someone who says, "You were great!" Someone who says, "You look great!" Someone who says, "Don't do it." A vividly bright yellow parakeet. The Chrysler Building on a rainy night. David Sedaris's audio recording of *Santaland Diaries*. **A good run,** physically or metaphorically. Leaving a party at precisely the moment you are having the most fun. Inge Morath's 1957 photo of that **llama in a cab** (google it), *A Llama in Times Square.*

Happy-making things in a difficult world:

Daffodils. Doing more with less. *Butch Cassidy and the Sundance Kid.* A pumpkin patch filled with screaming children. Going out to dinner the night before Thanksgiving. Whitney Houston's live version of "The Star-Spangled Banner." **A heart-shaped rock.** Late-afternoon Sunday drives. Christmas carols being played on a mildly untuned piano. Anything written by Judy Blume but especially *Blubber.* Lifting your arms into the air as the roller coaster ascends the big crest. A nail-biter of a [insert sport here] game. **Celebrating nurses** and the hard work they do, especially on the late shift. Frank Gehry's cardboard Wiggle Side Chair. A really chatty and supportive blackjack table. Billy Joel's recording of "Uptown Girl." **Knowing when you're done. Knowing when to keep going. Knowing when a pause is in order.** Miep Gies. A good friend who gives it to you straight. A squeaky porch swing on a cool summer night that you keep moving with the push of one big toe. Dionne Farris's recording of "I Know." **A tired, happy dog.** That moment when the entire movie theater explodes in simultaneous laughter. Herb Ritts's *Batman* photo. When someone lets you cut in line. Maurice Sendak's last *Fresh Air* interview where he says, *"Live your life, live your life, live your life."*

A freshly filled
sugar bowl.

Porcelain cow
creamers.

Happy-making things in a difficult world:

Old yellow NYC cabs. A sheet cake with neon-blue border icing. Yo-Yo Ma and the Goat String Quartet's recording of "Atta Boy" (play it today). Long strands of Spanish moss on an ancient live oak. **Wrigley Field.** A midday boat ride on a glass-smooth lake. **A late-night phone call with a friend** when it's blissfully quiet. The smack of flip-flops. Candice Bergen's autobiography, *Knock Wood.* Patty Duke's autobiography, *Call Me Anna.* Drew Barrymore's autobiography, *Little Girl Lost.* A pair of perfect creases on both sides of the present you're wrapping. Crisp, new sheets. The satisfaction that comes from shucking a basket of sweet corn. **People whose word is their bond.** Confetti. Seattle's Gum Wall. **Friends who are family. Family who are friends.** Turtlenecks. Gayle and Anthony and *CBS This Morning.* Robin and George and Michael and *Good Morning America.* Savannah and Hoda and *Today. When Harry Met Sally.* A sunken living room with a fireplace. The Supremes in general, but specifically their recording of "Love Child." Vintage Halloween decorations. **The Grand Ole Opry** when it's at the Ryman. A favorite photo of a loved one who is gone that you look at every day. Someone reading your palm. *Schoolhouse Rock!* Anne Tyler's novel *Dinner at the Homesick Restaurant.* Roseville pottery. A field of sunflowers. A murder of crows. The Nelson-Atkins Museum of Art in Kansas City. The song "Show Me Your Firetruck" from the *Backdraft* soundtrack. John Bryson's photo of Katharine Hepburn swimming in the Long Island Sound in February. Jimmy Fallon, national treasure. 125 years of *The New York Times Book Review.* Reduced expectations.

Happy-making things in a difficult world: A slow dance on a dimly lit porch. The moment before the giant bubble bursts. That August 12, 2020, *New York Times* article "The Pleasures of Moth-Watching" by Margaret Roach. **A working fireplace in the kitchen.** Annie Ross's recording of "This Time the Dream's on Me." Rotating the curtains. Gary Paulsen's *Hatchet.* E. B. White's *The Trumpet of the Swan.* Jacqueline Woodson's *Brown Girl Dreaming.* The fact that **the Eiffel Tower** can sway up to four and a half inches in a fierce wind. The fact that more than nine million people travel to **the Great Smoky Mountains National Park** in an average year, making it the most popular national park. The fact that cats sleep away more than half of the day. David Sanborn's recording of "Bang Bang." **Twizzlers. Junior Mints. Milk Duds.** Your diary's hiding place. Michael Nyman's score for *The Piano.*

Things You Might Consider Doing Today

Fastidiously make your bed. Dance to a ridiculous song such as "Rock Lobster" by the B-52s. Think about someone you've lost who meant a lot to you and then say their name loudly followed by "THANK YOU!" Lift someone up. Make a good sandwich and eat it slowly. Read Mary Oliver's poem "The Summer Day." Look at that incredible photo of Nixon and Elvis in the Oval Office. **Forgive someone who hurt you.** Give any amount of money to the charity of your choice in the name of someone else. Call a friend and don't use the pronoun *I* during the entire conversation. **Put your phone down.** Go outside and just sit and notice what's around you. Write down three things that make you happy. Watch an old movie you love. **Buy a book or two or four** or eight or sixty-four—you can order online or call your local independent bookseller. Send someone an anonymous gift. Listen to Beethoven's Ninth. Breathe deep. Exhale slowly. Hold someone's hand (that can include your own). Rinse and repeat after me:

"We will get through this.

We will get through this.

We will get through this."

Why Templeton Deserves
a Second Look

Charlotte. Wilbur. Templeton. These are the only three animals in E. B. White's *Charlotte's Web* that are named. While the other residents of the barn—the goose, gander, and various goslings, lambs, sheep, cows, horses, and swallows—form a sort of Greek chorus to the happenings in the book, just the spider, the pig, and the rat are fully formed characters. And if you haven't read the book in a while—or are lucky enough to have not yet read it—it's Templeton, the grouchy rat, who deserves a second look.

There is a certain fascination to be had of a grouch. The grouch is prevalent in popular culture: Oscar, of course, being the most famous, but also Old Man Marley in *Home Alone*, April Ludgate in *Parks and Recreation*, the main characters in *Grumpy Old Men*, Al Bundy in *Married . . . with Children*, Mr. Darcy in *Pride and Prejudice*, and Sophia Petrillo in *The Golden Girls*. The attraction isn't accidental; a "grouch" gives voice to our grumpiest thoughts, our bad moods, and the sometimes-wonderful pleasure of acting out whenever we want. A grouch presents the opportunity for us to live vicariously through someone else's bad behavior. And Templeton is no exception.

However, most of these grumps have an underlying, hidden decency (some admittedly more prevalent than others) that rises to meet the needed occasion. Such is the case with Templeton. Upon first encountering him, we learn that he is gluttonous, selfish, not-to-be-trusted, snippy, and merely a tolerated presence in the barn. Yet during the course of Charlotte's four miracles (it is still baffling that only Mrs. Zuckerman and Dr. Dorian focus on the wonder of the web and who wrote those four adjectives), Templeton's actions save the day five times:

1. It's the rotten goose egg that Templeton stored in the trough that scares Fern's meddlesome brother, Avery, from trying to capture Charlotte.

2. When Wilbur tries to make his own web, it's Templeton who both provides and ties the piece of starter string to Wilbur's tail.

3. Templeton initially balks at bringing a new word back from the dump for Charlotte, but after the sheep reprimands him and explains how his livelihood is connected to Wilbur's, the trip to the dump is confirmed. While Templeton's initial offerings of "Crunchy" and "Pre-shrunk" are reasonably rejected by Charlotte, the third time proves the charm with a bit of a soap flake box bearing "Radiant."

4. When Wilbur faints at the grandstand in the midst of getting his big prize, it's Templeton who sharply bites his tail and stirs him awake.

5. And finally, in his last gesture, which is done in the nick of time, Templeton refuses to remove Charlotte's egg sac—containing her five hundred and fourteen children—until Wilbur negotiates a deal (dinner first at the trough, and his choice of the feast). Yes, Templeton grumbles, negotiates, and complains that he's never thought of (not true), but in the end, he saves Charlotte's children and provides Wilbur with generations of friends. It should be noted that the grouch does *not* tell Charlotte goodbye.

Believing in (and appealing to) the best actions of someone should apply to grouches too, even though it's hard to see their goodness sometimes. Have you known a Templeton in your life? What act of kindness caused you to see them differently?

Before we got to know

the *Friends,* there was

thirtysomething:

Michael and Hope and

Nancy and Elliot and Gary

and Melissa and Ellyn.

Happy-making things in a difficult world: Philip Galanes's Social Q's column in *The New York Times*. **A vintage, crumb-free bread box.** A freshly painted crosswalk. A perfectly edged lawn. Monica's "COOKIE TIME" cookie jar from *Friends*. Melissa's winter coat covered in numbers from *thirtysomething*. Dre's sneaker collection from *black-ish*. That moment when the toys are all picked up and put away. Talking Heads' recording of "This Must Be the Place." Hitting the bull's-eye, literally or figuratively. **A romp of otters. A scurry of squirrels.** An unkindness of ravens. That November 19, 2020, Inspired Life article in *The Washington Post* by Paulina Firozi, "A Restaurant That Fed the Homeless Said It Might Have to Close. Donations Poured In." National Cheese Week. Buddy and Sally and Ben and Phyllis. That 1932 George Hurrell photo *Johnny Weissmuller*. Shaking the Etch A Sketch clear. **Striking the match and lighting the candle.**

Happy-making things in a difficult world:
Remembering that Ginger Rogers did everything Fred Astaire did . . . but backward and in high heels. Those moments when fewer supplies foster more inspired creativity. Bubble lights on a Christmas tree. Watching Ina Garten make anything. Paule Marshall's novel *Praisesong for the Widow*. **Dandelions that have gone to seed,** which you blow apart on a windy day. Someone saying, "Good morning!" Someone saying, "Wanna make out?" Someone saying and really meaning, "How are you today?" **A weighty, well-used cast-iron skillet.** Elizabeth McCracken's novel *The Giant's House*. Vacation rentals that feel so much like home, you're sad to leave. "Lowenstein, Lowenstein." Paper snowflakes you made as a child that someone saved. A long nap in a swinging hammock. The coo of a pigeon. The Menil Collection in Houston. The song "Maybe God Is Tryin' to Tell You Something" from *The Color Purple* soundtrack. Browsing the shelves of a bookstore (such as Three Lives & Company in Greenwich Village) on a weekend afternoon. The *SNL* digital short *Lazy Sunday*. When a friend brings you eggs from his chickens. Gilda Radner's audio recording of her autobiography, *It's Always Something*. Frosted strawberry Pop-Tarts. Nicknames that stick. **A small act of kindness that has a big impact.**

Happy-making things in a difficult world:

Calvin and Hobbes. Gordon and Kanin. Ennis and Jack. **The print edition of your local newspaper** waiting for you on your doorstep each morning. Kent Haruf's novel *Plainsong.* Arriving at a bucket-list destination. A bundle of nerves that someone puts at ease. The *Sesame Street* theme song. A really good brisket. Mastering the clap in the Go-Go's recording of "Head over Heels." A bowl full of dyed, pastel-colored Easter eggs. That moment when the groceries are all put away. WBGO's *Morning Jazz* (you can stream it). City hall weddings. Seating couples together at a dinner party. Fresh watermelon for dessert at the end of a long summer picnic. **Family movie night.** That YouTube video of "Uptown Funk" set to dance clips from old movies of the 1930s, '40s, and '50s. Williams. Federer. Williams. Seeing Seurat's *A Sunday Afternoon on the Island of La Grande Jatte* in person at the Art Institute of Chicago and being amazed at how big it is. **Yellow Peeps.** City parks. State parks. National parks. Animal rescue groups. Breakfast for dinner. The comfort of sitcoms playing in the background. A big, loud belly laugh that brings tears to your eyes. Edith Head's bangs. The Gamache novels of Louise Penny. **Turning up the volume all the way** when your favorite song plays on the car radio. The pop of a cork followed by a heartfelt toast.

Happy-making things in a difficult world:
Snoopy dancing. Andy Williams's recording of "Moon River." Barbara Jordan's 1974 impeachment speech. The big slide at the playground. *A Night at the Opera* starring the Marx Brothers. Ann Patchett's novel *Bel Canto*, especially the garden scene. A particularly vicious game of dodgeball. Six neatly stacked, unlit birch logs in the fireplace. The comic strip *Cathy* and the essay collection *Fifty Things That Aren't My Fault* by Cathy Guisewite. People who say, "Chin up!" People who say, "I hadn't thought of that." People who say, "Tell me more." Sharapova. Evert. Poodle skirts. Nureyev. Copeland. **A boiled egg whose shell peels off perfectly.** Hot-pink azaleas. Mastering the lyrics to Barenaked Ladies' "One Week." Emptying the piggy bank and rolling up the coins. Fresh-out-of-the-oven corn bread. Making that bucket list. Anne Rice's novel *The Mummy*. **Really good potato salad.** Louis Armstrong's recording of "Hello, Dolly!" The Brooklyn Bridge. The Golden Gate Bridge. The Stan Musial Bridge. Hitchcock in general, but specifically *Rear Window* and *To Catch a Thief.* The genius of Shirley Jackson's writing prowess. John Singer Sargent's *Portrait of Madame X.* The fact that Annie Proulx published her first collection of short stories at age fifty-three. Waiting up in anticipation for someone to come home from a long trip. An undulating field of wheat just as the storm comes in. Ladybugs. Good stationery. **The swagger of Indiana Jones.**

The fact that Michelle Yeoh used her own emerald ring as Eleanor's ring, which Nick uses to propose in the movie *Crazy Rich Asians*.

The fact that Grant Wood used his dentist and his sister as models for the farmer and his daughter in his 1930 painting masterpiece, *American Gothic*.

Happy-making things in a difficult world:

Waking up to snowfall. A jar full of multicolored glass marbles. Carly Simon's mash-up of "Coming Around Again/Itsy Bitsy Spider" from her *Live from Martha's Vineyard* concert album. The moment when you put on your pajamas. A red 1940s Ford truck. The sound of the Operation game buzzer. **Organizing the junk drawer.** The first bite into a ripe pear. The 11 o'clock number. Phone calls with friends that go late into the night. Perfecting a recipe that you later know by heart. The last page of Michael Cunningham's novel *The Hours*. The last page of Donna Tartt's novel *The Goldfinch*. The last page of Alan Bennett's novella *The Uncommon Reader*. Turning the last page of any book you are reading to/with a child at bedtime. Someone who says, "How are you feeling?" Someone who says, "Want some company?" Someone who says, "Wanna hear a secret?" A freshly clipped boxwood hedge. Marcella Hazan's tomato-butter-onion sauce recipe. **Agatha Christie novels.**

Junk food on a road trip. Ray Charles's recording of "America the Beautiful." Betty Ford, national treasure. Jimmy Stewart, national treasure. Oseola McCarty, national treasure (if you don't know her story, look it up). Those large pom-poms of allium. **A working Wurlitzer jukebox.** That Diane Arbus photo *Identical Twins, Roselle, New Jersey, 1967.* Sharing a heartbreak and feeling better afterward. The first bite of dessert. The walk through the woods up to Frank Lloyd Wright's Fallingwater.

Happy-making things in a difficult world:

The autumnal equinox. That 1978 Martha Swope photo *Ann Reinking in Rehearsal for the Stage Production "Dancin'."* That Mark Seliger photo *Central Park, April 7, 2020, 7:35 a.m.* That 1941 Marion Post Wolcott photo *Winter Visitors from Nearby Trailer Park, Picnicking Beside Car on Beach, Near Sarasota, Florida.* Jiffy corn muffin mix. **Early-morning quiet. Late-night quiet.** That moment when the quiet ends after a child's nap. The fact that the *Welcome Back, Kotter* theme song hit number one on the charts in 1976. The fact that Charles II declared that **six ravens must live at the Tower of London,** a tradition that continues today. The fact that the Vredefort Dome in South Africa is the world's oldest (at 2,023 million years) and biggest astrobleme. **The Library of Celsus.** That 1973 painting *Untitled* by Wifredo Lam. Growing a nest egg. Horton. Cindy Lou Who. The Lorax. Carol Burnett's autobiography, *One More Time.* Group hugs.

Happy-making things in a difficult world:

Knowing your limitations. Expanding your horizons. Helping someone else make their dreams come true. Cuff links. **A new pair of glasses that are a perfect fit.** Diane Keaton's crying jag in *Something's Gotta Give*. Diane Keaton's kitchen in *Something's Gotta Give*. **Keanu Reeves** in that blue T-shirt in *Something's Gotta Give*. A book recommendation from a friend that comes with the caveat "You'll either love it or throw it across the room." That April 30, 2019, *Washington Post* story by Elizabeth Evitts Dickinson, "The Case of the Stolen Ruby Slippers." That May 24, 2009, *New York Times* story by Larry Rohter, "Dear Donna: A Pinup So Swell She Kept G.I. Mail," about Donna Reed holding on to more than three hundred letters written to her from soldiers in World War II. That July 7, 2003, *New Yorker* story by Laura Hillenbrand, "A Sudden Illness." David McCullough, national treasure. The "Merry Christmas, Mrs. Moskowitz" episode of *Frasier* (season 6, episode 10). Wedgwood. **A group of people you love** singing "Happy Birthday" to you. Raw cookie dough. Terry Gross in general, but specifically her *Fresh Air* interview with Margo Martindale—you have to get all the way to the end, and before you do, get out the Kleenex. Rodgers and Hart. Rodgers and Hammerstein. Kern and Fields. **A train ride up the Hudson,** seated on the left side of the train so that you're closer to the water. Having an occasion that calls for using the good dishes. The shrieks of children on **the Tilt-A-Whirl** at a carnival.

"Carmina Burana."

The novels of Louise Erdrich.

The Chicago River turning green on Saint Patrick's Day.

Alanis Morissette's recording of "King of Pain."

Mount Rushmore.

Lisa Loopner and Todd.

Sitting on the front porch or steps
and watching the neighborhood pass by.

One of Ross Bleckner's *Falling Birds* paintings.

A game of catch in the backyard while the cicadas sing.

"Fasten your seat belts, it's going to be a bumpy night."

"If you build it, they will come."

"We're gonna need a bigger boat."

SPECIAL EDITION

The '80s

Happy-making things in a difficult world:

The eternal coolness of Molly Ringwald. Jake Ryan. *The Wonder Years.* Peeling the stickers off the Rubik's Cube and rearranging them to make it look as if you solved it. That moment after the new roll of Kodak film is in the camera. Goonies. **Having your parents drop you off at the mall** for hours with a prearranged pickup time. **Waldenbooks.** Montgomery Ward. Sears. *Bloom County.* Garfield sheets, comforter, and phone. Cathy and Irving. Sam and Diane. Regis and Kathie Lee. **Pay phones.** That red sweater with all the white sheep and the one black sheep that Princess Diana wore to Prince Charles's polo matches. The 1985 Chicago Bears. Steffi Graf. Katarina Witt. Anne Rice's novel *The Vampire Lestat.* Helen Hooven Santmyer's novel . . . *And Ladies of the Club.* Garbage Pail Kids trading cards. Gummy bears. New Coke. Wham!'s recording of "I'm Your Man." **Acid-wash jeans. Jordache jeans.** Oprah. Madonna. Cher (including the serious actress Cher). The Blue Moon Detective Agency. *"Where's the beef?"* Big hair. **Big shoulder pads.** Big eyeglasses. Speak & Spell. Ewoks. "I'll be right here." Janet Jackson's album *Control.* The debut of Julia Roberts in *Mystic Pizza.* That 1988 Annie Leibovitz portrait of Ella Fitzgerald in the red dress. Busy signals. Road maps. The heyday of newspapers, soap operas, and CODs. Talking Heads' recording of "Once in a Lifetime." Jimmy Stewart reading his poem about his beloved dog Beau and tearing up on *The Tonight Show*. Letterman. **Must-see TV.** Hallmark Hall of Fame. **Basquiat. Haring. Warhol.** Toni Morrison's 1988 Pulitzer win for *Beloved*. Wendy Wasserstein's 1989 Pulitzer win for *The Heidi Chronicles*. Elyse and Steven and Alex and Mallory and Jennifer. "Sit, Ubu, sit." The continuing, prolific output of Stephen Sondheim. Diane Schuur, national treasure. Michael J. Fox, national treasure. Elizabeth Glaser, national treasure. **Atari.** And because it bears repeating (and because he was born in 1980): Lin-Manuel Miranda.

Things You Might Consider Doing Today

Listen to that January 2009 *Fresh Air* interview with national treasure and hero Congressman John Lewis. Read that December 25, 2015, *New York Times* column by Jennifer Finney Boylan, "An Evergreen Tradition." Clean the grill. Dust the lampshades. Watch Jennifer Holliday's 1998 Carnegie Hall *Leading Ladies of Broadway* performance of "And I Am Telling You I Am Not Going." **Start a new craft.** Choose a photo for your holiday cards. Look at that 1924 Eugène Atget photo *The Pantheon*. Look at that 1909 Joaquín Sorolla painting *Walk on the Beach*. **Walk through the neighborhood** at a time you don't normally go out and see how different it looks. **Pick up some litter.** Google image search "Grand Teton + sunrise." Watch the 2004 video at the 58th Annual Tony Awards where Carol Channing and LL Cool J rap to "Hello, Dolly!" **Buy some fruit you don't normally eat** and then eat it. Make Martha Stewart's coconut cream pie recipe. If you are lucky enough to still be able to call your grandparents, call them. Crank "You Can't Stop the Beat" from *Hairspray* and start moving. **Offer a hand. Offer your time.** Take the long way home. Take a deep breath. Rinse and repeat after me: "*Hope begets further hope.*

Change begets further change.

Love begets further love."

Pause
and take a
rest today.

Happy-making things in a difficult world:
A meticulously ironed and buttoned-up powder-blue Oxford shirt.
Anne Tyler's novel *The Amateur Marriage.* **Someone who knits a hat for you.** Someone who makes you a perfectly proportioned mimosa on a Sunday morning. **Someone whom you happily let choose the movie.**
The Mighty Mighty Bosstones' recording of "The Impression That I Get." Snapping the container shut and putting it into the pneumatic tube in the bank drive-through. Lena Horne, national treasure. Michael Chabon, national treasure. Thomas Francis Jr., national treasure. That 1947 Felrath Hines painting *Two Heads.* Basket-weave tile. A hot fudge sundae with a cherry on top. A tightly packed bleacher filled with people you know. The fact that a praying mantis can rotate its head 180 degrees. *American Ninja Warrior. The Titan Games. Battle of the Network Stars.* Darren Criss's recording of "Teenage Dream." Sonny and Fredo and Connie and Michael. Game day. **Game night.** That moment when the streetlights click on.

Happy-making things in a difficult world:

Health-care professionals. Tony Bennett and Lady Gaga's duets album, *Cheek to Cheek*. The potential of a blank page, metaphorically or literally. Skeleton keys. A sporting event in which the underdog wins. That Jacques Lowe photo of JFK and Jackie eating at a diner during the 1960 campaign. Rob and Laura Petrie. The optimism of a kindergartner. Deviled eggs with paprika on top. A wicker basket on the front of **a vintage Schwinn.** An intense game of darts in a packed bar. The stand-up comedy of John Mulaney. Turning a decade number and embracing it. The films of Tim Burton, but specifically *Edward Scissorhands*. A child at a wedding/church service/serious, quiet moment who becomes bored, lets loose, and cracks the crowd up. LPs. Warm German chocolate cake. The twist in *Gone Girl*. The twist in *Presumed Innocent*. The twist in *The Secret History*. Pigs in a blanket. Friends of  friends who become your friends. Run-DMC's recording of "Walk This Way." Muir Woods. Someone who says, "Tell me something funny." *The Dick Cavett Show.* Chatty cabdrivers. Bright orange Nikes. *Fargo* (the movie).

A villain you find yourself rooting for.
Turning the other cheek. Linen napkins inside sterling silver napkin rings. The art of Edward Gorey, including the opening credits of *Mystery!* Maya Angelou's poem "And Still I Rise." Ordering off the menu. Hopscotch. A runny Popsicle on a hot summer day. **Rescue dogs. Rescue cats.** People who rescue dogs and cats. An album that evokes memories of a wonderful time in your life. The last dance of the night. Efficient meetings. Sunrise. A good suit. The promise of New Year's Eve after 10:30 p.m. Elaine Stritch's recording of "I'm Still Here." Hollyhocks. "Let's make it a true Daily Double." "Come on down!" "I'd like to spin." **Your heart on your sleeve, because how else should you wear it?**

Happy-making things in a difficult world:

Friday. White picket fences. The sound of surf coming in through an open window. The Pink Ladies. The Painted Ladies. The balconies on the Pontalba Apartments facing Jackson Square in New Orleans. **Using old photos as bookmarks.** Anne-Sophie Mutter playing Tchaikovsky's Violin Concerto in D. Growing up in a small town. That *Looney Tunes* cartoon where Bugs Bunny does the hair of the big red monster who says the most interesting things. Signing each individual library card with your full name when you checked out a stack of books as a child. Root-beer floats. **Movie night at a drive-in.** Riding the Staten Island Ferry and standing on the side that faces the Statue of Liberty. "Ditto." "After all, I'm just a girl, standing in front of a boy, asking him to love her." "That's your problem. You don't want to be in love, you want to be in love in a movie." That feeling of happiness you experience when someone tells you their good news. *The Paris Review* podcast. Double middle names. Someone who says, **"I believe in you."** Someone who says, **"You need to let that go."** Someone who says, **"You've crossed the finish line."** The novels of Fannie Flagg, particularly *Standing in the Rainbow*. Perfectly unwrapped and unbroken slices of Kraft Singles. Corgis. The Pretenders' recording of "My City Was Gone." The Red Room at the White House. That 2010 Snickers Super Bowl commercial starring Betty White. **Egg salad sandwiches.** Picking out your Halloween costume weeks in advance and changing it at the last minute.

The soundtrack from any John Hughes movie, but especially *Sixteen Candles*.

That smell when you pick a ripe tomato right from the stalk.

Joan Ganz Cooney.

Frank Oz.

Jim Henson.

Caroll Spinney.

The bouncy joy of Barbara Mandrell's recording of "Sleeping Single in a Double Bed."

A game of jacks.

Kit Kats.

Happy-making things in a difficult world:

Young Frankenstein. Getting through yesterday. *Pain au chocolat.*
Incredible feats of nature such as the three-thousand-mile migration
of the monarch butterfly. Denver's Union Station. Washington, DC's
Union Station. St. Louis's Union Station. The music of Eva Cassidy,
particularly her version of Sting's "Fields of Gold." Really good
meet-cute stories. Terrible date stories. That moment in dating life
when you trade keys. A terrifically juicy orange picked
straight from the tree. P.M. Dawn's recording of "Set Adrift on
Memory Bliss." People who start at a place of yes. People who operate in
a can-do manner. Miss Manners. Passing a note in class and getting
away with it. **The art of Louise Bourgeois.** Your
first crush. The Blues Brothers. Labor Day parades in small towns.
Freshly brushed teeth. **Jingles that you can sing
from memory,** such as "Plop plop / Fizz fizz / Oh, what a
relief it is!" Looking back at old diaries or journals and thinking, "Who
was that person?" Chicago's (the band) recording of "You're the
Inspiration." *Chicago* (the musical). Chicago's *Cloud Gate* sculpture
(The Bean). When you finally get the baby to sleep. Julia and Mary Jo
and Charlene and Suzanne and Anthony and Bernice. **The palm
trees that line Sunset Boulevard.** Barbara
Kingsolver's novel *The Poisonwood Bible.* Edie Windsor, national
treasure. Frances McDormand, national treasure. George Takai,
national treasure. That new car smell. That feeling when a new pair of
shoes are broken in. The way New Yorkers fold the print version of *The
New York Times* so as to not take up too much personal space on the
subway. Those fat bingo markers. Carnations. The Spiegel catalog.

Rural telephone party lines of the 1940s.

Happy-making things in a difficult world:

The Tanglewood music venue. Seven stories of New York Public Library books stored underneath Bryant Park. Staying positive as best you can. The whistle of a tea kettle. The sound of your best friend's voice. **First tries. Second chances. Third time being the charm.** The Nails' recording of "88 Lines about 44 Women." Warming up the car on a freezing-cold morning before you set out on the day. The acceptance of wrinkles and gray hair as badges of honor. Mary Murphy's PBS documentary, *Harper Lee: American Masters*. An old, threadbare, oval braided rug. The idea of breakfast in bed. The idea of a road trip. The idea of meeting your hero. Someone who says, "I don't know how you did that!" Someone who says, "I've done the 'ugly cry' too." Someone who says, "You are a marvel." The political perspective and wisdom of David Gergen. **Frozen margaritas, no salt.** Margaritas on the rocks, salt. Margaritas with friends on an early summer Friday afternoon. The old Yankee Stadium. The Green Monster. Yankees versus Red Sox. Annie Lennox's recording of "Georgia on My Mind." A tart, large slice of Key lime pie. The philanthropic work of Dolly Parton's Imagination Library. A really good, **lived-in pair of sweatpants.** Donating anonymously. Kathy Bates, national treasure. Diana Ross, national treasure. Johnny Mathis, national treasure. The satisfaction that arises from **ironing a shirt correctly.** Dipping in and out at any point in *The Andy Warhol Diaries*. Darning eggs. That first day of fall when you need to wear a jacket. **That first day of fall** when you can see your breath. Readily available Altoids. Ross and Rachel and Monica and Chandler and Phoebe and Joey. Funny aprons. Cattails. The act of moving forward.

Happy-making things in a difficult world:

That 2001 William Wegman photo *Twisted Hope*. The Apthorp. The San Remo. The Beresford. The old sweatshirt you love that you swiped from someone you dated and never returned. **Super Mario Bros. Space Invaders. Pong.** "My colors are blush and bashful." Acing the test. Barely passing the test and being happy with that. Bette Midler's recording of "Boogie Woogie Bugle Boy." Reba and Brock and Cheyenne and Van and Kyra and Jake and Barbara Jean. Gail Lumet Buckley's 2001 nonfiction, *American Patriots*. A game of four square on the **school playground at recess.** Recessed lighting. Double-lacing your favorite tennis shoes. The fact that Lucille Ball and Vivian Vance became **best friends in real life.** Green bean casserole. Perfectly chopping an onion. Your great-grandmother's cookie jar. That 1980 Seward Johnson statue, *The Awakening*, in Washington, DC. Someone who says, "Stop by anytime." Someone who says, "I'm going to check back on you." Someone who says, *"You should try this."*

The '80s, Part 2

Happy-making things in a difficult world:

Izod. Turned-up collars. *On Golden Pond. Jane Fonda's Workout.* Olivia Newton-John's recording of "Physical." Shopping for T-shirts and posters at Spencer's. Arcades. Glamour Shots. Goldie and Kurt. Wayland Flowers and Madame. Alice Walker's 1983 Pulitzer win for *The Color Purple.* Elie Wiesel's 1986 Nobel Peace Prize. Amy Tan's 1989 novel, *The Joy Luck Club.* **He-Man** and Battle Cat and **She-Ra** and Man-At-Arms and Skeletor and Castle Grayskull. *Big River. The Phantom of the Opera. Dreamgirls.* **Agassi. Agassi's hair.** The 1984 Boston Celtics. Watching Greg Louganis in the '84 and '88 Olympics and not knowing he would be a hero again soon for another reason. The heyday of *Life* magazine, catalogs, and *Reader's Digest.* That HBO logo ad that swept through that miniature town before the big movie began. *Ghostbusters.* That 1987 photo of Fergie and Diana poking people in the rear with their umbrellas at Ascot. **Floppy disks. CD players.** Teddy Ruxpin. "I'll have what she's having." "Bueller." The Bangles' recording of "Hazy Shade of Winter." Air Jordans. Larry "Bud" Melman. "No whammies!" Blanche and Rose and Dorothy and Sophia. Anita Baker's recording of "Giving You the Best That I've Got." Having your film developed. **New wave. Yoda.** *Teenage Mutant Ninja Turtles.*

Things You Might Consider Doing Today

Count your blessings. Crank "Bust a Move" and then do so. Do twenty-five push-ups. Do twenty-five sit-ups. Make Ina Garten's 1770 House Meatloaf recipe. Look up a few knock-knock jokes and share one. Start Patrick Rothfuss's The Kingkiller Chronicle series. Read Deb Perelman's article "How I Stock the Smitten Kitchen." **Scrub the bathtub.** Watch Margaret Atwood's 2020 Springsong/PIBO online gala. Find a stump and count the rings to discover the tree's age. Appreciate the passage of time. Stay in the moment. Watch *Wine Country* on Netflix. Start watching *Schitt's Creek*. Think about planting **some sort of garden.** Listen to those Carrie Fisher *Fresh Air* interviews. Express your devotion to someone who needs to hear it. Look through some childhood photos. Listen to Tierney Sutton's recording of "Old Devil Moon." Listen to Lou Gehrig's farewell speech. Send a note of encouragement. Look at that Tamara de Lempicka painting *Auto-Portrait (Tamara in a Green Bugatti)*. Expect more of yourself. Start doing what you want to do. And then rinse and repeat after me: "There is a lot of good in the world, even if I can't see it right now."

Small Towns

An after-supper trip to the Dairy Queen for a Dilly Bar. Church on Wednesday night, Sunday morning, and Sunday evening. Ball games, concerts, and school plays packed to the rafters with everyone you know. A casserole dropped off at a doorstop during a tough time with the owner's last name printed in block letters on masking tape stuck to the bottom of the dish.

There is a rhythm to a small town. The street grid might be smaller, but life happens just as fast and large and mercurial as anywhere else. Where I grew up, family, friends, kids, work, and church were the constants in life, as were holidays, the school calendar, and gossip. John Mellencamp croons about the epic scale of small-town life. And he's right.

There is a tendency for some people to think of rural life as simple; it's not. It is complicated, wonderful, messy, and heightened. But isn't that just life? Geography can define one's character and accent, but the experiences of life—the little moments that add up and become your story— play out for all of us in the same way, no matter where you live.

I've lived in a big city and a small midwestern town (Go Carterville Lions!), and I'm here to say that the similarities are as vast as the differences. In a city, the six-block radius surrounding your home is the heartbeat of your life. You have your dry cleaner, the bodega, your favorite restaurants, your routine, and the coffee shop where the barista starts your order the second you walk through the door. While you may not know the person who lives in the apartment next door, you do have a tribe, a work spouse, and lifelong friends. The same goes for a small town—it's just the space is wider, the sky more open.

There was a time when the television stations signed off with the national anthem; when you could dial the last four digits of a telephone number and reach your desired caller; and when back and front doors were never locked. The year I gave my grandparents an answering machine for Christmas, they made me take it back because they wouldn't use it. Save your money, they argued—if someone wanted to reach them, they'd just call back later or stop by. Why use a machine when human contact was the key?

That connection is the thread of small-town life. Help your neighbors. Support the fundraiser. Rebuild after the storm. Have faith. Ask questions. Don't put on airs. Family matters. Go the extra mile. Persevere quietly. Cheer loudly. Show up. Don't talk politics. Ask about the kids. Celebrate the holidays. All good advice to adhere to; a place and its people stay with you.

Have you ever lived in a small town? If not, what is your favorite small town to visit?

Someone who says,

"You've got something here."

⁓

Someone who says,

"Wanna dance?"

Happy-making things in a difficult world:

Miss Chanandler Bong. The Blues Brothers' recording of "Rubber Biscuit." The feel of the wind rushing through your hand hanging out the car window as you drive down a winding road. Picking out new school supplies. That March 4, 2009, *All Things Considered* story, "After 66 Years, Veteran Reunited with Dog Tag." Andrew Young, national treasure. Dominique de Menil, national treasure. Isaac Stern, national treasure. The tradition of burying the bourbon. That 1934 Barbara Hepworth sculpture, *Mother and Child*. That 1971 Geoff Winningham photo *Tag Team Action, Houston Wrestling*. That 1954 Victor Brauner painting *Prelude to a Civilization*. Carol and Harvey and Vicki and Tim and Lyle. **Margaret Atwood's Twitter.** The rattle of the metal ball in a spray paint can when shaken. The fact that on a clear day you can see four different states from the top of the Willis Tower. Pocket doors. Hot Pockets. A pocket full of posies. Lea DeLaria's recording of "I Can Cook Too."

Happy-making things in a difficult world:

Morning dew on the grass. The wit and wisdom of Carrie Fisher. Sharing a buttery bucket of popcorn at the movies. R.E.M.'s recording of "Stand." **Bowling shoes.** The worlds created by Erin Morgenstern. Celia and Marco. Zachary and Dorian. Orchids you manage to keep alive and in bloom. An early start to the workday. **Chess sets made up of fictional characters,** such as the Simpsons. NPR's *Wait Wait . . . Don't Tell Me.* Dried hydrangeas that keep their shape. The fact that the Chagall murals commissioned for the Metropolitan Opera were hung in the wrong spots. A bunch of lit votives as a table centerpiece. A particularly vehement book club discussion. Cleaning out the lint trap. Pugs. Home games. Away games. That 1952 diamond Cartier panther bracelet made by Jeanne Toussaint for the Duchess of Windsor. **A good plumber. A good contractor. A good line,** such as Groucho Marx's "I've had a perfectly wonderful evening. But this wasn't it." Guests who arrive right on time. Easily forgiving guests who arrive late and putting them at ease. Old hardware stores. The Statler Brothers' recording of "Flowers on the Wall." **Subway station performers** playing Mozart. Jean Stapleton, national treasure. Jessye Norman, national treasure. Charles Schulz, national treasure. Biscuits and gravy. Bus drivers who wave to pedestrians. **The babble of a brook.** The ceiling of Grand Central Terminal. Drinks at the Campbell Apartment in Grand Central Terminal. The Whispering Gallery at Grand Central Terminal. Nick and Nora and Asta. Murray's Cheese. Anything from Zingerman's. A budding weeping willow. Someone who brings you chicken soup when you need it. Someone who says, "Get some rest." Someone who says, "Sit tight." The comfort provided by a softly glowing night light. A small box of Ladurée macarons.

Happy-making things in a difficult world:

A spiral-bound church cookbook that contains one of your grandmother's recipes. Peter Lefcourt's novel *The Dreyfus Affair*. Standing at the top or bottom of San Francisco's Lombard Street and watching the traffic wind down. Someone who says, **"I've done worse."** Someone who says, **"I've seen worse."** Matching turquoise Vespas. Crepe myrtle in full bloom. Jimmy Durante's recording of "Make Someone Happy." The terrific noise of a packed playground. Heated towel racks. **Driving the Blue Ridge Highway.** Jackalopes. Kaleidoscopes. Sea monkeys. Funny airline attendants. The art of David Hill. Doing the wave in a packed stadium. The Westminster Dog Show. The Beekman Mercantile. **Tea at Harrods.** José Andrés, national treasure. Tina Turner, national treasure. Frances Perkins, national treasure. The glow of birthday candles. **Blowing out the birthday candles. Getting the first slice of cake.** Built-in bookshelves. Natalie Cole's recording of "Orange Colored Sky." The architecture of downtown Milwaukee. **The Twitter account of *Atlas Obscura*.** That "Peter Comes Home" Folgers coffee commercial. That 1981 Peter Hujar photo of Madeline Kahn. *Dirty Dancing. Strictly Ballroom.* Warm pecan pie. The fact that people used to get dressed up for the theater. A cocktail at the King Cole Bar at the St. Regis. Tandem bikes. Dre and Rainbow and Zoey and Junior and Jack and Diane and Devante. The entire score of *The Pajama Game.* Slug bug. That sound when you sink a shot in air hockey. **Paddleboats. Steamboats. Dreamboats.**

Happy-making things in a difficult world:

Taking the leap. That feeling when you wake up on the first day of vacation. Andra Day's recording of "Rise Up." Snowfall in December. Gus the polar bear. *CBS Sunday Morning*'s "Moment of Nature." **A field of Muscari.** Melissa McCarthy, national treasure. Susan Zirinsky, national treasure. Toni Morrison, national treasure. That photo of Toni Morrison dancing. During hard times, the thought of "When everything gets back to normal I am going to . . ." Dunking an Oreo in a glass of milk until it becomes a bit soft. **Photos of Halston** at Studio 54. Donna Summer's recording of "I Feel Love." Cagney and Lacey. Burns and Allen. Ashford and Simpson. Woody and Buzz. The Plaza in Kansas City. *The Runner* sculpture in Athens. Doris Kearns Goodwin in general, and specifically her masterpiece of nonfiction *No Ordinary Time*. The work ethic of Robert Caro. Frances Glessner Lee and *The Nutshell Studies*. The Kennedy Center Honors and the fact that the recipients do not give speeches. **Kids selling lemonade in their driveways.** Backyard barbecues. Nine-on-nine volleyball games. Family reunions where everyone wears a matching T-shirt. Old John Deere tractors. The Vermont Country Store. Christopher Kimball's *The Yellow Farmhouse Cookbook*. Mini-corn-shaped corn-cob holders. CorningWare. Tupperware. The Philippe Starck juicer. Kristin Chenoweth's recording of "Taylor, the Latte Boy." **Faith in yourself.** Faith in **someone else.** Your favorite book as a child. *Sleepless in Seattle. Down with Love. She's All That.*

Vintage pinball machines. Vintage merry-go-rounds. Vintage thrift shops. Stopping at the top of the Ferris wheel with someone you love and seeing the night lights in the distance.

Happy-making things in a difficult world:

Cherry blossoms. Blossom Dearie's recording of "Rhode Island Is Famous for You." **A full moon on a clear night.** A cord of freshly stacked firewood. A jolt of confidence when you need it the most. **Cake walks.** That Slim Aarons 1957 New Year's Eve photo *The Kings of Hollywood.* Having someone's expectations of you be not only met but surpassed. Having a day you can fully shape for yourself. When something just clicks into place. Good knife skills. Relay races. Potato sack races. The exhilaration of the fifty-yard dash. Philip Johnson's Glass House. The Rothko Chapel in Houston. The infinity mirror rooms of Yayoi Kusama. Punctuality. The whisper of pine trees in the wind. Witty, yet thoughtful toasts to the bride and groom. The prize at the bottom of the cereal box. Danny Glover, national treasure. Dr. Mathilde Krim, national treasure. Dorothy Hamill, national treasure. When your kids fall asleep on the car ride home. Someone who says, **"Don't worry about that."** Someone who says, **"Take your time."** Someone who says, **"After you."** Don and Betty and Roger and Bert and Peggy and Joan and Pete. Your favorite coffee mug. A busy hotel restaurant at breakfast. Epistolary novels, such as *The Guernsey Literary and Potato Peel Pie Society* by Annie Barrows and Mary Ann Shaffer. Grocery store workers. Yaz's recording of "Only You." Copper pots hanging together on a kitchen rack. A new pair of Gingher scissors. An unopened box of unsharpened pencils. **The dog run.** Breakfast nooks with built-in seating. Mending something that needs to be mended. The friendship between Mike Mulligan and Mary Anne. Fresh mulch. **Clean eyeglasses.** *Waiting for Guffman.*

Gomez and Morticia and Wednesday and Pugsley and Uncle Fester and Grandmama and Lurch and Cousin Itt and Thing.

That "Boiling Oil" cartoon of the Addams family standing on the roof just about to tip a full cauldron onto unsuspecting carolers at the front door below.

Things You Might
Consider Doing Today

Make pancakes. Make a "To Be Read" pile. Make a batch of sun tea.
Watch BBC broadcaster Andrew Cotter's "annual report" Zoom video
with his dogs. Watch P!nk's live performance of "Glitter in the Air"
from the 2010 Grammys. Scrub the grout. Line the cabinets. Clean
the screens. Meet someone where they are, not where you want them
to be. Listen to Patrick Radden Keefe's podcast, *Wind of Change*.
Have a picnic. Take a nap outdoors. Take the "Rijksmuseum
Masterpieces Up Close" virtual tour. Read Jeff Gordinier's April 2014
New York Times article, "Laurie Colwin: A Confidante in the Kitchen."
Stop checking email. Look at that 1967 David Hockney
painting *A Bigger Splash*. Organize your medical and financial records.
Send a valentine. Leave the Hallmark Channel on all day. Blast Melissa
Manchester's recording of "You Should Hear How She Talks About
You." Realize that changing your life is possible. Purge the closet.
Consider the alternative. **Make a different choice.**
Watch Mel Brooks's *High Anxiety*. Hug a little tighter. Take a moment.
And then rinse and repeat after me:

"Today is a good day."

A to Z

Happy-making things in a difficult world:

Aperitifs at 11:00 p.m. **B**ackup plans that are rendered unnecessary. **C**lose-ups of your favorite movie star. **D**riving the Pacific Coast Highway at dusk. **E**veready batteries at hand in whatever size you need. **F**ocusing on the task at hand as if your life depended on it. **G**utting the pumpkin while watching *Garfield's Halloween Adventure*. **H**and quilting. **I**mmersing yourself in a sunken, bubble-filled tub. **J**ohn F. Kennedy Jr. playing touch football in Central Park. **K**itchen talk with a friend during a busy holiday gathering. **L**ast chances that bear fruit. **M**aking the most of an unpleasant situation. *Nancy Drew and the Secret of the Old Clock*. **O**beying the rules and then breaking them because they were wrong. **P**urple martins. **Q** *is for Quarry*. **R**equesting your favorite song at a dance and hearing it minutes later. **S**pontaneous classroom laughter. **T**aking someone's dream seriously. **U**nder-the-bed storage. **V**anquishing a long-held fear. **W**atching a scary movie with a group of friends. *Xanadu*. **Y**our favorite smell. **Z**ero regrets.

Romy and
Michelle.
Benson and
Stabler.
Titus and
Kimmy.

MIXTAPE:
Chin Up, Young Person

Guess what? I made you a mixtape.
This one is for a good day to keep
you moving, or for a bad day to cheer
you up. Feel free to shuffle, but please
begin with the first song, Ella Fitzgerald's recording of "Blue Skies," because it's amazing. Now hit Play. And then go tell someone how much
they mean to you. And then think about how glorious this beautiful,
messy life can be. And then make it a good day.

A	B
"Blue Skies" –Ella Fitzgerald	"Kind & Generous" –Natalie Merchant
"Sir Duke" –Stevie Wonder	"Maybe God Is Tryin' to Tell You
"Rhode Island Is Famous for You" –Blossom Dearie	Something" –*The Color Purple*
"Nessun Dorma" –Aretha Franklin	(Original Motion Picture
"Out of My Head and Back in My Bed"	Soundtrack)
–Loretta Lynn	"Rhapsody in Blue" –Andre Previn, Piano
"Better Get to Livin'" –Dolly Parton	"Head over Heels" –The Go-Go's
"Sit Down, You're Rockin' the Boat"	"Uptown Funk" –Mark Ronson and
–*Guys and Dolls* (1992 New	Bruno Mars
Broadway Cast Recording)	"Rock Lobster" –The B-52s
"Uptown Girl" –Billy Joel	"Hello, Dolly!" –Louis Armstrong
"Skylark" –Aretha Franklin	"Ode to Joy" –Beethoven
"Atta Boy" –Goat String Quartet	"One Week" –Barenaked Ladies
"Lazy Sunday" –The Lonely Island	

Happy-making things in a difficult world:

Suspension bridges. A boisterous dinner party without leftovers. Making the best of a bad day. March Madness. Milk in glass bottles. Someone who says, "There's time to fix it." Someone who says, "You can do better." Empathy for those who are carrying something heavy inside (in other words, all of us). **Leather passport cases.** Agent Cooper. Agent Scully. Agent Mulder. Hot-air balloons rising in the sunrise. Bette Midler's recording of "Chapel of Love." **Fried chicken sizzling in a cast-iron skillet.** An old, much-loved quilt. The underground indoor pool at San Simeon. The outdoor pool at San Simeon. Pool noodles. Joseph Nye Welch, national treasure. Arthur Ashe, national treasure. Laurie Metcalf, national treasure. *The Four Freedoms* series of paintings by Norman Rockwell. Making friends with people you meet on vacation. The intricate masonry of the Alwyn Court building. Old home movies that show long-lost loved ones laughing and smiling. A summer day spent outdoors with **a giant doorstop of a novel,** such as *Jonathan Strange & Mr Norrell* by Susanna Clarke. A cold winter's night spent in front of a crackling fire with a giant doorstop of a novel. Standard poodles. Irish setters. Earth, Wind & Fire's recording of "September." An energetic, educated, and engaged docent on a museum tour. Those red British telephone booths. That Eudora Welty photo *Delegate, Jackson, Mississippi, 1938.* The Chihuly ceiling at the Bellagio in Las Vegas. Funny key rings. The fact that Michael Curtiz directed both *Casablanca* and *White Christmas.* Plump footstools. **Pen pals.** Leonard and Penny and Sheldon and Amy and Bernadette and Howard and Raj. SMEG refrigerators. Refrigerator magnets. **A child's art on the refrigerator.**

Happy-making things in a difficult world:

Your favorite coffee shop. The hiss of the espresso machine. Venus flytraps. Anna Quindlen's nonfiction *A Short Guide to a Happy Life.* A waffle-knit bathrobe one size too big. Puddles of syrup in your waffle. **A full schedule. A free day.** Playdates. *Bridesmaids.* Three-piece suits. A pocket watch with an engraved message on the casing. That 1943 Weegee photo *The Critic.* Someone who knows when to push. Someone who knows when to back down. Running up the seventy-two steps at the entrance of the Philadelphia Museum of Art and doing the Rocky pose at the top. Jadeite pottery stacked in a cupboard. An unexpected flower delivery. **A Dutch door** with the top open. Harry James's recording of "I've Heard That Song Before." Homemade Halloween costumes. *Wit,* the Pulitzer Prize–winning (and, to date, only) play by Margaret Edson. A perfectly executed layup. That moment just before the cereal turns soggy. Yo-yo quilts. Rolling out the pie dough perfectly. Exposed brick walls. **Shadow puppets. The Muppets.** Firehouse dogs. The fact that President Woodrow Wilson turned on the lights of the Woolworth Building in NYC in 1913 by pushing a button in Washington, DC. Laura Branigan's recording of "Gloria." *People* magazine's cover story. Opening and believing in all of the **fortune cookies** that come with your Chinese food takeout. Madeleine L'Engle, national treasure. Jane Mayer, national treasure. Gene Wilder, national treasure. **The joy of speculating** the motive behind and solution to a great mystery, such as the robbery of the Isabella Stewart Gardner Museum in Boston. Lucy and Ethel. Rhoda and Mary. Will and Jack. Little girls with pigtails. Keeping it together. Letting it all hang out. Having a stiff upper lip.

Happy-making things in a difficult world:

Riding the wave, figuratively or literally. Worn-out driving gloves. Putting on a fresh pair of socks after an evening run. That 1940 Ellison Hoover lithograph *Snowstorm at the New York Public Library*. That October 7, 2016, *Atlas Obscura* article by Sarah Laskow, "Inside the New York Public Library's Last, Secret Apartments." Anchor Hocking blue bubble Depression glassware. **Your collection of** [insert what you love and collect]. Barbra Streisand, national treasure. John Doar, national treasure. Ed Bradley, national treasure. John Coltrane's recording of "My Favorite Things." The moment the snoring stops. The fact that an elephant's ear is nearly six feet long and five feet wide on average. McDonald's Happy Meal toys. Acadia National Park. Someone who says, "Here is what you are going to do." Someone who says, "Take it easy." Someone who says, "Spill it." The Sanderson Sisters: Winifred, Sarah, and Mary. **A giant bouquet of Queen Anne's lace in a vintage pitcher**.

Thanksgiving

Happy-making things **in a difficult world:**

Stuffing. Hosting. Not hosting. A drive without traffic. Falling asleep in the back seat. That moment **when the last anticipated family member arrives.** That moment when Santa arrives in the Macy's Thanksgiving Day Parade. Watching the Macy's Thanksgiving Day Parade floats chart north on Columbus Avenue the night before Thanksgiving and hearing the jingle bells on Santa's sleigh. "The Wheel" episode of *Mad Men* (season 1, episode 13). **Family photos.** Weather-beaten mums. Turkey-shaped place cards made from the template of a child's hand. **Seeing cousins you haven't seen in a while.** Throwing all the coats on the bed in a pile. All the pies. All the sides. Candied yams with walnuts on top. The fancy tablecloth. Water goblets. Holiday sweaters. Awkward conversations. Asking your senior relatives about their childhood and **hearing a story you've never heard before.** Unexpected connections. Coffee after dinner. Touch football after dinner. Cards after dinner. Carols after dinner. Carols on the radio. Naps. Currier and Ives. Singing "Over the River and Through the Woods" at top volume. Secrets shared. Heading out to the movies. Staying home to watch the *National Dog Show*. **Silently remembering those who've passed** and missing them tremendously. Stepping outside to cool off, figuratively or literally. Snoopy serving up popcorn, jelly beans, sundaes, and buttered toast. The ending of *Planes, Trains, and Automobiles*. Decorating the tree after dinner. **Leftovers for dinner.**

MIXTAPE:
Bubble Lights on the Christmas Tree

A little holiday music for the season to help you celebrate, decorate, or zone out from the madness of December.

"Christmas Dinner, Country Style" –Bing Crosby

"Light One Candle" –Peter, Paul, and Mary

"Christmas Wrapping" –The Waitresses

"Ring Christmas Bells" –The Ray Conniff Singers

"With Bells On" –Dolly Parton and Kenny Rogers

"The Christmas Song" –Ray Charles

"Christmas Is" –Lou Rawls

"I Believe in Father Christmas" –Greg Lake

"Song for a Winter's Night" –Sarah McLachlan

"I Like a Sleighride (Jingle Bells)" –Peggy Lee

"Christmas Moon" –Jackie Gleason (not a typo)

"What Christmas Means to Me" –Stevie Wonder

"Christmastime for the Jews" –TV Funhouse and Darlene Love (*Saturday Night Live*)

"Winter Wonderland" –Harry Connick Jr.

"The Night before Christmas" –Carly Simon

"Step into Christmas" –Elton John

"Do You Hear What I Hear?" –Pink Martini

"Winter Wonderland" –Eurythmics

"The Chanukah Song" –Adam Sandler

"I'll Be Home for Christmas" –Nancy LaMott

"Auld Lang Syne" –Mairi Campbell

Stringing popcorn for the Christmas tree.

Things You Might Consider Doing Today

Connect. Make that phone call. Eat dinner by candlelight, but eat dessert first, and play some Billie Holiday while you do (*Lady in Autumn: The Best of the Verve Years*). Clean out your spice rack. **Look at some old pictures** that bring back happy times. Start organizing the photos in your phone into digital albums. **Play a game of Scrabble.** Watch the "Job Switching" episode of *I Love Lucy* (season 2, episode 1). Throw out that book you can't get into and start a new one. Send three postcards to someone you love that separately say "I" and "LOVE" and "YOU!!!!" Give an hour to yourself. Plan what you will do this Fourth of July, end of summer, Halloween, Thanksgiving, and at the holidays. Think about trying something new. Look at that 1932 Berenice Abbott photo *Nightview, New York.* **Go outside at dusk and listen to the birdsong.** Make someone laugh. Read Mary Oliver's poem "The Uses of Sorrow." **Fix something that needs to be fixed.** Listen to Gilda Radner's recording of "Let's Talk Dirty to the Animals." Give your pet some extra treats. Drop off a small gift at your neighbor's front door and don't ring the bell. Move forward, but keep looking back in that rearview mirror to remember how far you've come. Rinse and repeat after me:

"It's never too late."

Dream big.

Wish big.

Love big. ♡

Think big.

Happy-making things in a difficult world:

Dinah Washington's recording of "I'll Remember April." Junie B. Jones. Anastasia Krupnik. M. C. Higgins. The smell of crayons when you open a new box. **The day they finally fill the pothole.** Jesus Jones's recording of "Right Here Right Now." The fact that snowflakes aren't white but instead clear, and it's the reflection of light that causes their white or blue hue. That 2020 Bisa Butler fabric artwork, *The Warmth of Other Suns.* Peter and Andrew and Carol and Roger and Mary and Sarah and Brian and Maggie. The entire soundtrack to *The Big Chill.* Glenn Close, national treasure. Angela Bassett, national treasure. Allison Janney, national treasure. Two magical, retired jersey numbers: 42 (baseball) and 23 (basketball). **The squishiness of a marshmallow.** The gooeyness of a warm mozzarella stick. The stickiness of a bear claw doughnut. That August 12, 2017, article in *The Guardian* "Shelf Life: Novelist Hanya Yanagihara on Living with 12,000 Books." And because it bears repeating: Lin-Manuel Miranda (and Alexander's dance of joy when Eliza's father gives his marriage blessing in "Helpless").

Happy-making things in a difficult world:

An organized sewing box. Hostas. Russell Wright's 1939 "American Modern" pottery line in the color "granite." Wrist corsages. Top hats. *Top Gun*. The monthly Good Dog column in *Garden & Gun* magazine. Florence + the Machine's recording of "Shake It Out." The annual NASA Earth Day poster. The family piano. Seeing someone you love all dolled up. That Mark Seliger photo of the *Seinfeld* cast dressed as *The Wizard of Oz* characters. Finding a photo of your grandparents when they were young. The delight in jumping around in the Choose Your Own Adventure novels. The 1982 St. Louis Cardinals. The Saturday night *Svengoolie* classic horror movie. Sunday afternoon naps. Someone who says, "Hang in there." Someone who says, "Wanna go to the movies?" Someone who says, "Name one good thing that happened today." Riding in the bed of a pickup truck with the wind making a mess of your hair. A freshly squeegeed windshield. Sidney Bechet's recording of "Si tu vois ma mère." Alison and Billy and Michael and Jane and Jake and Jo and Matt and Sandy and Rhonda and Kimberly and Sydney. African dwarf frogs. Steve Martin's album *Comedy Is Not Pretty!* A warm pepperoni pizza. Cold leftover slices. John Williams, national treasure. Jane C. Wright, national treasure. Dorothy Parker, national treasure. Comic books shared between you and a child. The unexpectedly deep thoughts of an eight-year-old. Sponge curlers. Wind chimes that aren't annoying. Jeff Koons's *Puppy* sculpture. Accordions. Hope springing eternal.

Happy-making things in a difficult world:

Bobbing for apples. A happy message on a dry-erase board. That 1958 Art Kane photo *A Great Day in Harlem.* Someone who says, "That's a good idea." Someone who says, "You look great!" Someone who says, "What are you doing today?" Jonathan Larson's *Rent.* Those little cans of Farrow & Ball paint samples. A royal blue AGA stove. **An assortment of ranunculus** wrapped in butcher paper for sale at a farm stand. Auli'i Cravalho's recording of "How Far I'll Go." The costume designs of Theoni Aldredge, specifically for *The Great Gatsby.* The fact that Fitzgerald wrote the manuscript for *The Great Gatsby* in pencil, in longhand, and on typewriter paper. The "corner portraits" of Irving Penn. Winning the ring toss and taking home a goldfish. Bowie's German recording of "Heroes." Softly melted mini-marshmallows in a giant mug of hot chocolate. Friendship between cousins. Apple-red Adirondack chairs surrounding a lit outdoor firepit. A mahogany 1950 Chris-Craft Sportsman boat. The 2016 Chicago Cubs. A stroll through the Portland (Oregon) Japanese Garden. Depeche Mode's recording of "Just Can't Get Enough." A pile of leaves ready to be jumped into. The very good work of Share Our Strength. The ground-floor Art Deco men's bathroom at Nashville's Hermitage Hotel. The novels of Miss Read. **Bear hugs.**

A day at the state fair.

Corn dogs.

Cotton candy.

Funnel cakes.

Happy-making things in a difficult world:
The way small children end up playing with the box instead of the
gift. The Eames Lounge and Ottoman, 1956. The Mies van der Rohe
Barcelona Chair, 1929. The Marcel Breuer Wassily Chair, 1925.
A steak and a Scotch at Smith & Wollensky. Amanda
Gorman, national treasure. Rosa Parks, national treasure. Lily Tomlin,
national treasure. Meerkats. Baby chimpanzees. Someone who says,
"You can get through this." Someone who says,
"Well, what are you waiting for?" Someone who
says, **"Just jump in feetfirst."** The art of Charlie
Mackesy. A pressed flower that you kept to remember the reason behind
the arrival of the flowers as well as the person who sent
them. That 1994 Norman Mailer *Esquire* interview with Madonna.
Tonka trucks. That 1966 Harry Benson photo of Mia Farrow and Frank
Sinatra in their masks at the "Black and White Ball" thrown at The Plaza
by Truman Capote. The short stories of Lorrie Moore. The Crystal
Bridges Museum of American Art. Flying kites on a windy beach. The
fact that **art, music,** TV shows, **books, films,**
dance, **and love** can be passed from generation to generation.
Pat Benatar's recording of "We Belong." Thick wool socks on a chilly
night. Danner Jag boots. Kurt and Blaine. Mitchell and Cam. Villanelle
and Eve. That moment when you know it's going to be a home run,
literally or figuratively.

Happy-making things in a difficult world:
Blossom Dearie's recording of "Unpack Your Adjectives." Tuxedos.
Going barefoot in the uncut summer grass. **The art of browsing** and then finding something you had forgotten you needed. That Howard L. Bingham photo *James Meredith, Mississippi Civil Rights March, 1965.* Robert and Cora and Mary and Edith and Sybil and Branson and Violet and Isobel and Matthew and Carson and Mrs. Hughes and Anna and Bates and Barrow and O'Brien and Daisy and Mrs. Patmore. **"Mind the gap."** The promise of a gap year. Kate Bush's recording of "Running Up That Hill." That moment when you see the person coming to pick you up round the corner. That moment when **you reach the summit** after an arduous climb, literally or figuratively. That moment after **you pick yourself up,** dust yourself off, and start all over again. That 1962 Elizabeth Catlett sculpture *Seated Woman.* Boris Aronson, national treasure. Tharon Musser, national treasure. Gregory Hines, national treasure. Neuschwanstein Castle. Maleficent's Castle. The fact that Bram Stoker was the manager of **London's Lyceum Theatre** for twenty-seven years. James Marsden's teeth. Julia Roberts's laugh. Caroline Fraser's Pulitzer Prize–winning history, *Prairie Fires: The American Dreams of Laura Ingalls Wilder.* The fact that **the deepest known part of the ocean** in the Mariana Trench, "Challenger Deep," is nearly seven miles in depth. The fact that the red sea urchin resides solely in the Pacific Ocean, and those in Canada can live for more than two centuries.

Happy-making things in a difficult world:

Handbell choirs. Hand-lettered invitations. Kids in school uniforms. A 1971 MGB convertible. **That moment after a storm** when the clouds break and the sunshine has a strange, glowing hue. Henry Mancini's recording of "Baby Elephant Walk." Deadlines. The writers of the headlines of the *New York Post*. **Someone who saves you a plate.** Someone who does the late-night walk with the dog. Tony Kushner, national treasure. Lynn Nottage, national treasure. Tracy Letts, national treasure. Making friends with your seatmate when traveling, all the while knowing you may never see each other again. The Harry S. Truman Presidential Library and Museum, Kansas City. Flowering cyclamen. Pi day. A journey on the Belmond British Pullman train. **Sleeper cars.** That cable-knit sweater Chris Evans wore in *Knives Out*. Michelle Pfeiffer's Catwoman costume. **To-do lists.** X-ing off the current day on the calendar in the morning with high hopes. Al Green's recording of "Let's Stay Together." The first night you spend in a new home. Aaron Rodgers and the 2011 Green Bay Packers. **The forty thousand basalt columns that make up the Giant's Causeway.** "They call it a 'Royale with Cheese.'" That 1971 Ron Galella photo *Windblown Jackie*. Little Edie. Big Edie. *Big Night*. Helping with a child's science project late into the night. Doing the crossword in ink. The fact that Harry Winston donated the Hope Diamond to the National Museum of Natural History in 1958 and sent it via registered mail. The first three Dragonlance novels. Carrie and Miranda and Charlotte and Samantha. **Nachos.** Listening to the song of life.

That Moment in Your Life When You . . .

Took a solo drive in your first car. Could accurately thump a melon. **Stopped saying yes when you meant no.** Survived a bad haircut. Survived a broken heart. Fell on the sword. Mended a fence. **Built something for yourself.** Won big. Faced a loss with grace. Saw the world in a different way thanks to an incredible teacher. Turned a bad vacation into an unforgettable vacation. Realized your parents are people too. Realized that other people's priorities were not necessarily your priorities. Tapped a keg. Did karaoke unabashedly. Ignored a wise suggestion from an elder that you knew was true but you didn't want to accept, so you didn't do what they said you should do and had it all blow up in your face, and then you trusted said elder implicitly thereafter. Bowled a turkey. Snuck out of the house. Got that big promotion. **Moved on without a glance back.** Took that big trip. Showed a child *The Wizard of Oz* for the first time. Saw *The Rocky Horror Picture Show* at a midnight screening. Celebrated Mardi Gras in NOLA. Stepped up when no one else would. Learned that regret is useless except as education. Saw that first gray hair. Discovered your favorite author. Discovered your favorite album. Opened your own bank account. Ran a marathon, literally or figuratively. Recognized the fact that going to bed early is fantastic.

Started doing that thing you always teased your parents about doing, like double-checking the lock or being extremely concerned about changing air filters. Got through a bad home renovation. Hit the big 3-0. Went to your first concert. Decided on "your song" as a couple. Valued someone else's time. Valued your own time. Learned that keeping secrets is no small matter. Did that thing that terrified you. Changed someone's mind.

Things You Might
Consider Doing Today

Start a jigsaw puzzle. Stay in your pajamas. Mop the kitchen floor. Crank Stevie Wonder's recording of "Sir Duke" and start dancing. Request a catalog from White Flower Farm, even if you don't have a yard. **Pick a ridiculous word**—say, *haberdashery*— and try to work it into your next conversation. Skip the news. Watch a basketball game. Watch Seth Meyers's comedy special, *Lobby Baby*. Watch clips of Jonathan Winters on *The Tonight Show.* **Help someone else.** Read David Sedaris's 2019 *New Yorker* piece "Hurricane Season." Look at Nicholas Nixon's four decades' worth of photographs of the Brown Sisters (October 3, 2014, *The New York Times*). Make Alison Roman's sheet cake with mascarpone and coffee. Take a virtual tour of Santa Fe's Georgia O'Keeffe Museum. Listen to Susannah McCorkle's recording of Jobim's "Waters of March." Stop worrying about your hair. **Find a new podcast.** Set the alarm in order to get up in time to watch the sunrise tomorrow. Keep looking for the helpers. **Walk the dog a little bit longer.** Don't feel bad for eating that candy. If you're going through a bad time, think about what it will feel like when it is over. Think about how glorious and magical life can be. Now take a deep breath. Rinse and repeat after me:

"Superheroes can be everyday heroes."

Grandfather clocks that have a rich hand-me-down story.

Live Like Mary Bailey

There's a reason the movie *It's a Wonderful Life* has played on television for years and become a part of the holiday tradition and psyche: transformation. George's salvation is the engine of the film, as potent and lasting as Scrooge's. But if you watch the movie closely, something else is also happening.

As the movie progresses, specifically with the dance at the gym, you begin to see that it's Mary Bailey, time and time again, who is the real hero. Yet for Mary, transformation isn't her North Star; rather, it's a firm belief in herself. She is a person who Gets. Things. Done. Ah, but George lassos the moon, you say! Yes, but ever-steady and ever-ready Mary lassos life. The movie is hers. Played with smarts, determination, and grace by the one and only Donna Reed, it is Mary's stalwart, all-American resolve that anchors the film. It is a wonderful life, and Mary shows us exactly how in ten steps:

1. **Know what you want.** Think of the soda fountain scene where young Mary leans over and whispers into young George's ear, "George Bailey, I'll love you till the day I die."

2. **Have a vision and turn it into a reality.** Mary knows that someday she'll live in the Old Granville House and makes that her wish as she and George throw rocks at the broken windows.

3. **Make the best of a bad situation.** With zero help from George *at all*, Mary creates an entire honeymoon suite and dinner on their wedding night.

4. **Sacrifice reaps dividends.** As George tries to calm the crowd after the stock market crash, it's Mary who offers up their savings to keep the building and loan—and townspeople—afloat.

5. **Do it yourself.** We see Mary wallpaper and refurbish the Granville house to its former glory, with the exception of the newel post.

6. **Keep dancing when things go wrong.** If the gym floor ever opens up beneath you and you find yourself immersed in a pool, just keep dancing.

7. **Do not covet what others have.** Sam Wainwright's fancy car, chauffeur, big job, and glamorous girlfriend register no impact on Mary when they show up to the Martini house blessing.

8. **Spring into action when things get tough.** Once George storms out of the house after realizing the money is gone, Mary immediately picks up the phone to call Uncle Billy, and later we realize she's sent a telegram to Harry *at the White House* asking him to come home.

9. **Celebrate with abandon.** In the last scene, as the town comes pouring into the Bailey home, it's Mary who says, "Mr. Martini, how about some wine?"

10. **Have faith, but believe in yourself—and others.** As the money piles on the table, Uncle Billy tells George, "Mary did it, George!"

I have known several Mary Baileys in my life. My best friend's mom, Pam Finley. My mother-in-law, Dolores Losapio. My stepmom, Patti Doughty. Both of my grandmothers, Evadean Church and the late, the great, the pistol, Peggy Doughty. Our neighbor Pat Broadbent. My mom.

Who is the Mary Bailey in your life? When have you lived like Mary Bailey?

Happy-making things in a difficult world:
Subway's $5 Footlong. Carvel's Fudgie the Whale cake.
Shake Shack's Egg N' Cheese. That August 31,
2020, *Washington Post* article by Sydney Page, "How This Former
Doctor Ended Up Flying Thousands of Dogs Across the Country to
Save Them." **A box of untangled paper clips.**
Perfectly aligned wooden hangers.
Calaveras Big Trees State Park, once home to the Tunnel Tree.
The 7,392 feet that make up the Baltimore Harbor Tunnel. John Waters,
national treasure. Sonia Sotomayor, national treasure. Beverly Johnson,
national treasure. **Ice that is thick enough to skate**
on. Alexander Liberman's 1950 painting *Two Circles*. The Louisville
Slugger Museum and Factory. Wilson baseball gloves. Rounding third
and heading home. Multiple flower arrangements on the dinner table.
Kim Carnes's recording of "Bette Davis Eyes." George and Martha
and Nick and Honey. The old Magnolia Bakery. "The first rule about
fight club is you don't talk about fight club."

John Legend,
national treasure.

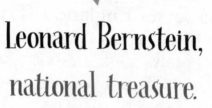

Leonard Bernstein,
national treasure.

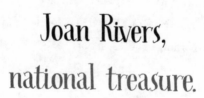

Joan Rivers,
national treasure.

Things You Might Consider Doing Today

Make some finger puppets inspired by your favorite fairy tale and then put on a show. Google image search "Everglades + sunset." Dive into *Garden & Gun*'s online celebration of Julia Reed's most popular columns, "The Indelible Voice of Julia Reed." Move a lamp to a different spot in the living room. **Search on YouTube for Diego Maradona's goal in the 1986 Argentina versus England FIFA World Cup match.** Read that August 29, 2020, story "What Bread Tasted Like 4,000 Years Ago," by Keridwen Cornelius and Sapiens, posted on *The Atlantic* online. Look at that 1963 Wayne Thiebaud painting *Jawbreaker Machine*. Listen to the audiobook of Frank Langella's memoir, *Dropped Names: Famous Men and Women as I Knew Them*. Wipe down the inside of the microwave. Read Ken Liu's incredible 2011 short story "The Paper Menagerie." **Finish that thing you've been meaning to finish.** Listen to Eartha Kitt's recording of "C'est si bon." Recognize that sometimes just getting through the day is more than enough. Smile.

MIXTAPE:
Need a Jolt?

Kick-start the day, or restart the day, or reset the day with this jolt of a playlist. Make it a good day for yourself and for someone else. Feel free to shuffle, and happy listening.

A	B
"Always on My Mind" –Pet Shop Boys	"Generals and Majors" –XTC
"Better Be Good to Me" –Tina Turner	"Dreamlover" –Mariah Carey
"Devils Haircut" –Beck	"Sugar" –Maroon 5
"My Baby Just Cares for Me" –Nina Simone	"Beast of Burden" –Bette Midler
"Ants Marching" –Dave Matthews Band	"Shut Up and Dance" –Walk the Moon
"Buddy Holly" –Weezer	"Happy" –Pharrell Williams
"Sowing the Seeds of Love" –Tears for Fears	"I Want It That Way" –Backstreet Boys
"America" –Neil Diamond	"You Don't Know" –Cyndi Lauper
"I Say a Little Prayer" –Aretha Franklin	"Would I Lie to You?" –Eurythmics
	"Blister in the Sun" –Violent Femmes
	"Stand" –R.E.M.

Happy-making things in a difficult world:

Having a pot-filler faucet over the stove. Mudrooms. Cubbyholes. **Green Hunter Wellington boots.** Peter Lik's photography. Buying flowers for your mother. John Mellencamp and Me'shell Ndegeocello's recording of "Wild Night." Cafe Luxembourg. Accepting that nothing is perfect. Art as comfort. Music as comfort. **Food as comfort.** *The Love Boat.* The Yellowstone Caldera. That 1928 black-and-white Eugene Robert Richee photo of Louise Brooks and her strand of pearls. The 1999 FIFA Women's World Cup and that photo of Brandi Chastain celebrating the win. Kander and Ebb, national treasures. Huntley and Brinkley, national treasures. Kathy Najimy and Mo Gaffney, national treasures. *Amadeus.* The stillness that accompanies early-morning fog. Your first kiss. Your first Broadway show. Bernadette Peters's recording of "Move On." A homemade valentine. Calla lilies. Moving day. Reflecting. A heavy pour of Justin Cabernet. A good bartender. A night out on the town. Washing the dishes together after a family dinner and sharing a private joke. A Coleman lantern. *Take Me to the World: A Sondheim 90th Birthday Celebration.* **Someone who leaves a light on for you.** Someone with a big heart. The Grinch.

Happy-making things **in a difficult world:**
Snood hairnets from the 1940s. Skinny ties. Skinny Pop. OshKosh B'Gosh overalls on a toddler. Simon and Garfunkel's recording of "Cecilia." Linda Eder's recording of "Bridge Over Troubled Water." The day the training wheels come off your bike. **The day the braces come off your teeth.** The day when you can do something for your parents. A variety of choices on the coatrack. **Being the first one on the dance floor** and then drawing others onto the dance floor. The Thymes Frasier Fir Pine Needles candle. The Votivo Red Currant candle. Kirstie Alley's 1991 Emmy speech. A sensory memory that hits you out of the blue. That Henri Cartier-Bresson quote via Cardinal de Retz, "There is nothing in this world that does not have a decisive moment." That 1941 Yousuf Karsh portrait of Winston Churchill. **A parliament of owls.** The entire *O Brother, Where Art Thou?* soundtrack. Lorraine Hansberry, national treasure. Harvey Fierstein, national treasure. Jason Collins, national treasure. Tony and Carmela and Meadow and A.J. and Christopher and Adriana and Junior and Livia and Paulie and Dr. Melfi. A salt pig next to the stove. A game of Parcheesi. **A roll of the dice,** literally or figuratively. Oliver Peoples eyeglasses. Rankin/Bass. Integrity. Charity of spirit.

Happy-making things in a difficult world:
Piccolos. Rain falling on a tin roof. Three-quarter-sleeve T-shirts. Glass half full. Baby grand pianos with framed family photos covering the lid. Herringbone-pattern floors. Vince Guaraldi Trio's recording of "Linus and Lucy." **A Sunday stroll along a waterfront.** That story of how John D. Rockefeller Jr. bought the Palisades to protect his view of the Hudson. The Little Red Lighthouse under the George Washington Bridge. Window seats. That Harold Edgerton 1957 photo *Milk Drop Coronet.* The eighty-one houses scattered across the Thimble Islands off the coast of Connecticut. **Winter cabbage.** Graduation day. McCoy pottery. Someone who says, **"Keep at it."** Someone who says, "What do you mean you've never seen [insert classic movie]? We have to fix that!" Someone who says, "Make it better." Acts of political courage. Oasis's recording of "Wonderwall." **Making someone who doesn't laugh easily laugh.** Walkie-talkies. R. J. Palacio's novel *Wonder.* The Thorne Miniature Rooms at the Art Institute of Chicago. The entrance to Grove Court in Greenwich Village. A patterned fire screen. Alice Ball, national treasure. Hattie Caraway, national treasure. Sharon Olds, national treasure. **The Zen of a Zamboni.** "Buffalo gals won't you come out tonight, and dance by the light of the moon?" "You had me at hello." **"Help me, Obi-Wan Kenobi. You're my only hope."** Warm coffee cake.

Happy-making things **in a difficult world:**

A sink full of billowing soapsuds. That March 5, 2018, article by Chloe Shaw in *The American Scholar*, "What Is a Dog?" That moment when a dog you don't know **flops over for belly rubs.** Ribsy. Sounder. Old Dan and Little Ann. Perfectly twisting the spaghetti onto your fork without the aid of a spoon. Rachael & Vilray's recording of "I Love the Way You're Breaking My Heart." Paisley Park. Graceland. Six friends squeezing into a table for four. Brandi Carlile's recording of "The Joke." Waking up three minutes before the alarm goes off. Ariel Lawhon's novel *Code Name Hélène*. Jennifer Tipton, national treasure. Annette Gordon-Reed, national treasure. Bob Mackie, national treasure. Kadir Nelson's 2020 painting *After the Storm*. Vacation rentals with an outdoor shower. A work of art that passes the Bechdel test. Breakfast on the go. Nancy LaMott's live recording of "Secret O' Life." Katharine Hepburn's 1991 autobiography, *Me: Stories of My Life.* Sharing the armrest. A driver who slows down and allows you to merge easily. That moment after the garage door fully closes. **Throw pillows with surprising or cheeky needlepoint sayings on them,** such as "If you can't say anything nice about anybody, come sit by me." Calphalon. All-Clad. Watching the pot and seeing it boil. Mash notes.

IF YOU CAN'T SAY ANYTHING NICE ABOUT ANYBODY, COME SIT BY ME

An overflowing magazine rack at the dentist's office that presents myriad reading options.

Happy-making things **in a difficult world:**
The gingham-lined bread basket at the restaurant. The opening chords of "Seasons of Love" from *Rent.* **That sneaker squeak on the basketball court.** Rocky and Bullwinkle. **Shaggy and Scooby-Doo.** Fred and Barney. That new-eraser smell. Connecting the dots, literally or figuratively. That 1945 Lee Miller photo *Irmgard Seefried, Opera Singer Singing an Aria from* Madame Butterfly. Someone who says, "Try again." Ryan Murphy's *Feud.* Show and tell. **That moment after the air horn stops.** John Peterson's The Littles. Deborah and James Howe's *Bunnicula: A Rabbit-Tale of Mystery.* Gertrude Chandler Warner's The Boxcar Children. **Knowing that late is better than never.**

Happy-making things in a difficult world:

A tarnished copper weather vane. Perusing the Balsam Hill catalog. Girls' night out. Adele's recording of "Water Under the Bridge." The Pont Neuf. June Cleaver's pearls. Lady Gaga's soda-can hair rollers. Eddie Murphy's laugh. Successfully completing the assembly of [insert child's toy]. **Successfully flipping the omelet. Successfully avoiding the squeaky stair.** A rusty but functioning door knocker. Adding a dash of cinnamon to the coffee grounds. That April 24, 2017, *New Yorker* profile by Ariel Levy, "Elizabeth Strout's Long Homecoming." Beverly Sills, national treasure. Marilynne Robinson, national treasure. Luis Miranda, national treasure. **Scritti Politti's recording of "Perfect Way."** The fact that it can take ten years for some species of magnolia trees to bloom. The fact that some species of centipedes can live for five years. The fact that the distance between the pitching mound to home plate is sixty feet, six inches. That 1910 Umberto Boccioni painting *The City Rises*. Mary and Lester and Brenda and Rose Lee and Tiffany and Pearl and Sandra. Shuffling through a carpet of colorful leaves. People who don't keep score. Someone who keeps you company in the kitchen while you cook. Someone who gives you your space, no questions asked. Someone who makes it work in spite of seemingly insurmountable odds. That 1960 Getty Images / Metropolitan Museum of Art photo *Guests at the Fashion Ball*. **Almond Joy.** Mounds. Butterfinger.

"Kevin!!!!"

A leap of leopards.

A charm of finches.

A stack of quarters to fill an afternoon at the batting cages.

That moment when the heartache stops.

Patience and Fortitude.

Personalized bookplates.

And because it bears repeating: Lin-Manuel Miranda (and his June 19, 2014, *New York Times* essay, "Pursuing the Muse Against the Clock").

Summer

Memorial Day is the traditional start of summer, but it's not until the last day of school passes that the season truly begins. There is a freedom and sense of escape associated with summer that continues long into adulthood.

That endless stretch of summer opens wide before you, soon to be filled with long, hot days and (hopefully) cooler nights where the sheet is needed, not discarded in a heap at the end of the bed.

The grill is fired up, and you eat on the deck. Surf and turf is a possibility; potato salad becomes an essential food group. A fiercely competitive game of horseshoes is played on the lawn. The garden grows out of control. Fresh peaches need to be savored and canned for winter.

Trips are planned and taken. You visit the beach, or the backyard kiddie pool, or the mountains, or the lake, where you can run on a long deck, jumping in feetfirst with your arms held high. You decide what tune is going to become your "song of summer."

You pack into a cool theater to see the summer blockbuster on opening day. Tiki torches dot the yard. Wet swimsuits dry on the back of patio chairs. Fireflies rest in the palm of your hand.

Summer is a time of celebration, its fleeting nature to be cherished (not a bad metaphor for life in general either).

What is your favorite "song of summer"? What summer activity did you love to do most as a child?

Things You Might
Consider Doing Today

Make Ina Garten's lasagna with turkey sausage (vegetarian substitution in recipe). Buy a new pair of sweatpants in a ridiculous color. Resolve to finish the crossword. **Make a playlist of your favorite songs** from college. Call someone you haven't spoken to in a long time. Call your local bookstore, say you'd like to place an order, give them your budget and favorite genre, and tell them to surprise you. Work the phrase "You know, I never thought that [insert huge hit sitcom] was that funny" into a conversation just to see what happens. Turn the TV off and leave it off. **Write your hero a fan letter.** Read Robert Fulghum's essay "All I Ever Really Needed to Know I Learned in Kindergarten." Do something selfless. Blast Aretha Franklin's recording of "I Say a Little Prayer." Look at that Pete Souza photo of John Travolta dancing with Princess Diana at the White House. Close your eyes and think about your favorite book as a child. Flip the mattress. Remember the first teacher who believed in you. Send some pizzas to your local hospital's nurse station. Weed the front sidewalk. Check out what the New York Philharmonic is streaming. Watch *Raiders of the Lost Ark* and *Indiana Jones and the Last Crusade* and then pretend the other two movies in the series don't exist. Refold all of the towels. Remain optimistic, like a kid who is ready for a big test. **Google "Alexander Calder + circus."** Explore the digital exhibitions of the Smithsonian's National Museum of American History. Start making plans: Who will you visit? Where will you go next? When will you make that change you've needed to make? How will you move forward? How will you reach out to others? Then take a deep breath. Rinse and repeat after me: *"You can accomplish a lot in a single day."*

Yard sales
at which
you discover
something
valuable.

On Summer Reading

For me growing up, summers always meant time to read with abandon. Once I was old enough to stay home by myself, I had a long-established routine. At 9:00 a.m. I washed whatever dishes were in the sink while watching *Live with Regis and Kathie Lee*, mesmerized by the eighteen-minute discussion of their previous evening's doings in New York. Then I'd start laundry in the basement, blast Captain and Tennille's *Song of Joy* album while vacuuming, and finish whatever else needed to be done—all so that by 1:00 p.m., the afternoon was freed up for me to do nothing but read.

I come from a long line of voracious readers. My papa was a coal miner who took a book with him on that long elevator shaft ride down each day; he devoured everything from Shakespeare to Stephen King. My uncle Dennis reads everything but has a specific affinity for nonfiction, particularly history and biographies. Once, after I visited him in Houston, he sent me home with a duffel bag filled with books he thought I should read. And my mom reads for at least an hour before bed each evening—she and my stepdad are regulars at the Anne West Lindsay Library.

In the library of my youth there was a bell on the door, the cool air and quiet quickly enveloping you the moment you entered after the jingle. The magazine rack and card catalog were on your right, children's section on your left, the check-out desk dead center, and stacks beyond. The amazing librarians were always at hand, ready with a recommendation; the kids' summer reading program was legendary (you signed up, and for each finished book, a star was placed next to your name); and you could request articles on any subject, copied by a county librarian and assembled into a packet that arrived days later. It was pure escape, and there was no greater thrill than being the first person to check out a book.

A few pivotal summer reads: Reading the complete Wizard of Oz series by L. Frank Baum as a kid; sneaking home Judy Blume's *Wifey* as a preteen; trying (and failing) to grasp Salman Rushdie's *The Satanic*

Verses at age fifteen; and spending days in the hammock outside our trailer in college devouring Anne Rice's *The Witching Hour* in its weighty trade-paperback form during my senior year at Southern Illinois University. The bigger the doorstop, the better the book.

What book has been a favorite summer read for you? What did your childhood library look like?

Happy-making things in a difficult world:

The Dells of the Wisconsin River. The buildings of McKim, Mead, and White. Popcorn balls. Naming all fifty states from memory. Naming all fifty state capitals from memory. When the storm passes, literally or figuratively. **Piggyback rides.** Someone who says, "Just give it a try." Someone who says, "Cut bait." Someone who says, "Give me a hug." **A packed picnic table.** The Matisse collages at MoMA. Duct tape. The nineteenth hole. Keeping your word. Fender guitars. Roxy Paine's steel tree sculptures. Your childhood lunch box. The last school bell of the day. The story behind that 1933 Dorothea Lange photo *White Angel Breadline*. Statement necklaces. Fleece pullovers. A sunny day in London. That first sip of morning coffee. **That first sip of wine at 5:01 p.m.** Stacey Kent's recording of "So Many Stars." A starry night. The historic 1930s subway "Holiday Nostalgia" line. That 1952 Raymond Gosling photo *Photo 51*, which helped identify the structure of DNA. Susan Stamberg, national treasure. Diana Nyad, national treasure. Jon Bon Jovi, national treasure. Jake and Amy and Captain Holt and Terry and Rosa and Gina and Scully and Hitchcock and Charles. Nora Ephron's essay collection *I Feel Bad About My Neck*. **The glow of the fridge when searching for a midnight snack.** Sitting on a blanket under the Fourth of July fireworks. Sitting on a beach at sunset and feeling the sand between your toes. The opening and closing credits of *Alfred Hitchcock Presents*.

Things to Look Forward To

Flying home and seeing your parents waiting for you in the baggage claim. In-person author events. Hearing a crowd of fifteen hundred people in the theater cheer together at the end of the 11 o'clock number. **People-watching in an extremely busy hotel lobby.** Singing along to "Sweet Caroline" at Fenway. Saving the ticket stub. **A boring day in the office.** Crossing that thing off the bucket list. Dancing to Stevie Wonder's "As" in a large group. Betty White's hundredth birthday. Browsing. **Commuting. Meetings in person.** Dinner with friends in a crowded restaurant. A slow news cycle. Margaret Atwood's **new short story.** John Grisham's **new novel.** Annette Gordon-Reed's new nonfiction. Kadir Nelson's **new painting.** Annie Lennox's **new album.** Tony Kushner's new play. Wes Anderson's **new movie.** Tyler Mitchell's **new photo**. A Saturday movie matinee with the beverage and snacks of your choice and an engaged audience. **A ridiculously fashion-filled red carpet.** A digitally restored print of *The Lion in Winter*. Going to the opera for the first time. Early lost recordings of Whitney Houston. That new thing that brings you joy and then you tell someone about it and then it brings them joy. Uninterrupted glee. A worry-free day. Science embraced at large. Concerts. Hugs. Handshakes. Necessary trouble. Reaching the other side of something challenging (which you will!).

Happy-making things in a difficult world: Colson Whitehead winning the 2020 Pulitzer Prize in Fiction (his second) for *The Nickel Boys*. Bauman Rare Books. Elvis Costello and the Attractions' recording of "Pump It Up." Steaks cooked to the temperature of your choice. The waiters and ordering process at Peter Luger. Lingering over that one last drink after the check arrives. **A Sidecar. A Manhattan.** A Bee's Knees. That moment when the jackhammer stops. A tree-lined driveway that forms a natural cathedral of sorts. Filter's recording of "Take My Picture." Hasselblad cameras. Photos of your parents in high school. The art of Tug Rice. Your favorite summer job. Snow cones in July. The CBS Sunday Night Movie. *Monday Night Football.* **Cheering someone on.** Cheering someone up. Encouragement. Marble countertops. **Push-button light switches.** Weekend travel. Susan Minot's novel *Evening*. Geoff Ryman's novel *Was*. John Berendt's nonfiction *Midnight in the Garden of Good and Evil*. The Jack Leigh photo *Bird Girl*, which was used on the *Midnight in the Garden of Good and Evil* cover. **Pay day,** literally or figuratively. Your coziest sweater. Your favorite, worn-out ball cap. "If you can dodge a wrench, you can dodge a ball!" Tony and Angela and Sam and Jonathan and Mona. Someone who says, "Cheers to you!" Someone who says, "I knew you could do it!" Balloon animals. Party favors. Bursting the piñata.

Happy-making things in a difficult world:

Going through the car wash. A vacation sunburn. A vacation romance.
Hotel room service. Potbellied stoves. Irons in the fire. Bananarama
and Fun Boy Three's recording of "It Ain't What You Do."
Having the remote control all to yourself.
That 1943 photo of Louis B. Mayer and all the MGM stars in which
Katharine Hepburn is the only woman wearing pants. The story
behind Bob Gruen's 1974 photo of John Lennon in the "New York City"
T-shirt. The story of how Random House editor Bob Loomis
persuaded Maya Angelou to write *I Know Why the Caged Bird Sings*.
The hum of the cables that run San Francisco's cable
cars. Pitching in. Opting out. Someone who says, "Why not?" Someone
who says, "You're a lifesaver." Cicely Tyson, national treasure. Jonas
Salk, national treasure. Tennessee Williams, national treasure.
The Super Bowl. The underground vault at the National
Archives that houses the "Charters of Freedom" each night.
The U.S. Postal Service. Carefully tended stamp
collections. Dick and Joanna and Stephanie and Michael and George
and Larry and Darryl and Darryl. Andrew Wyeth's painting *Master
Bedroom*. Weeding the garden. **Planting your flag.**
Changing the scenery. Stove Top stuffing. Etta James's recording of "A
Sunday Kind of Love." The Neighborhood of Make-Believe. "Look, I
made a hat."

Happy-making things in a difficult world:

A KitchenAid mixer complete with attachments. Apple corers. Carrot peelers. Snapping green beans. Andy Goldsworthy's natural sculptures, particularly *Storm King Wall*. Sweet tea. The October 1978 issue of *National Geographic* that featured Koko the gorilla's self-portrait on the cover. **The "pop trash" mosaic art of Jason Mecier.** Saddle shoes. Hush Puppies. Carly Simon's recording of "I'd Rather It Was You." The Jimmy Stewart Museum in Indiana, Pennsylvania. The fact that Jimmy Stewart sent his Oscar to his dad in Indiana, Pennsylvania, to be displayed in the front window of the family hardware store. **The entire score of Gershwin's *Porgy and Bess*.** Accepting your flaws. Denying your fear. Kate Christensen's novel *The Great Man*. Stephen McCauley's novel *The Man of the House*. Isabel Allende's novel *The House of the Spirits*. Shredding documents you no longer need. The quiet before the drumbeat in Whitney Houston's recording of "I Will Always Love You." Drinks after work. The Budweiser Clydesdales. Listening to the Cardinals game on KMOX radio. Dinner with friends. Having dinner on a rooftop at sunset with a chill in the air. Short grocery lines. Archie and Edith and Gloria and Michael. Cutting out coupons. The 2004 Red Sox comeback against the Yankees in the ALCS. "There's no crying in baseball!" **The entire score of *Avenue Q*.** Stomping in puddles.

Happy-making things in a difficult world: Choosing your battles. Gossip. **The balloons in the Macy's Thanksgiving Day Parade.** The aesthetic of Wes Anderson. A funny pair of dress socks that peek out when you sit down. Having intentions and following through. The New York Public Library. Christopher Milne's original **Pooh and friends stuffed animals** at the New York Public Library. Bogie and Bacall. SJP and Matthew. Bert and Ernie. Nina Simone's recording of "April in Paris." Someone who says, "I already took care of that." Someone who says, **"You get me."** Someone who says, **"Call anytime."** That feeling when you lift a tray of honeycomb out of a beehive and it's vibrating with the bee's energy as they continue to move about. *The Far Side.* Opening a jar of home-canned peaches in the middle of winter and making a cobbler that reminds you of summer. The Chicks' recording of "Landslide." **Reading a bunch of magazines** on a long flight and then giving them to the flight attendants. Biltmore. The ridiculous requests of every potential home buyer on *House Hunters.* Bruce Springsteen's recording of "Glory Days." That Richard Avedon photo of the model and the elephants. Paul Zindel's novel *The Pigman.* Going out on Saturday night to the newsstand across the street from your apartment to get the early print edition of the Sunday *New York Times.* The Rolling Stones' recording of "You Can't Always Get What You Want." First editions. Pennies on the train tracks. **People who decorate for fall.**

The art of Al Hirschfeld. Believing someone when they show you who they are. Sally Ride, national treasure. Shirley Caesar, national treasure. Robert Ballard, national treasure. "Have fun storming the castle!"

Reese's peanut butter cups.

Happy-making things in a difficult world:

Someone who picks you up, literally or figuratively. The final lap around the track. "Big mistake. Big. Huge. I have to go shopping now." That December 1, 2018, *Time* magazine piece by Jon Meacham, "George H.W. Bush Believed in the Essential Goodness of Americans." The Kohler Whitehaven undermount single-bowl farmhouse kitchen sink. The Perrin & Rowe Georgian Era Bridge kitchen faucet. The Philippe Starck Peltoo spatula. Ernie's recording of "Rubber Duckie." **Refilling the ice cube tray without spillage.** Guinness World Records. Chadwick Boseman, national treasure. Helen Rodríguez Trías, national treasure. That 1941 Gordon Parks photo *Sleepy Time.* **Walking through Christo and Jeanne-Claude's *The Gates* sculptures in Central Park, 2005.**

Squeezing too many people into the diner booth. Spreading out a towel on the beach, soaking up some sun, and then taking a nap before high tide.

Alice and Flo and Vera and Mel and Tommy. Tennessee Williams's *Cat on a Hot Tin Roof.* A sleuth of bears. A troop of kangaroos. A warren of rabbits. The fact that Pluto is 3.1071 billion miles away from Earth. That 2017 Amy Sherald painting *What's Precious Inside of Him Does Not Care to Be Known by the Mind in Ways That Diminish Its Presence (All American).*

Bucket-List Suggestions

Happy-making things **in a difficult world:**

Hear "Rhapsody in Blue" performed live. Learn French. Learn how to cook an elaborate dinner for twelve. Host a perfect dinner party after cooking said dinner. Chaperone your niece's or nephew's school dance. See the brilliance of *Hamilton* again in the theater. **Own a bicycle again.** Own a piano again. Go to the [insert your town's name] opera. Go to the Grand Ole Opry at Christmas. Attend *Saturday Night Live* (the 11:30 p.m. live show, not the rehearsal). Organize a literacy charity event. See Lady Gaga in concert. **Visit Paris in April.** **Read all of Jane Austen's novels.** Read all of the Robert Caro LBJ biographies and *The Power Broker.* Travel to Normandy, Africa, Machu Picchu, the Anne Frank House, Prague, and a Red Sox–Yankees game at Fenway. Meet three of your personal heroes. Visit Page & Palette, Literati, and Prairie Lights bookstores. Visit the Mount. **Witness a *Sound of Music* flash mob.** Adopt a rescue dog, preferably an Irish setter. Get a living legend's autograph. **Get back to a place you love** that you haven't been to in a while. In life, embrace each "new" normal as it arrives.

Happy-making things **in a difficult world:**
The fact that George Gershwin began writing "Rhapsody in Blue" on January 7, 1924, and the piece premiered in New York on February 12, 1924, with the composer at the piano. Ben Platt's recording of "Somewhere." Matching thumbtacks. **Looking for the name you need in the lobby directory and finding it quickly.** A decent passport photo. Eydie Gormé and Steve Lawrence's recording of "Black Hole Sun" (you're welcome). Dr. Ruth Westheimer, national treasure. Danny Thomas, national treasure. Sheldon's spot. Adrienne Gaffney's September 2, 2020, *Town & Country* article, "A Debutante Delayed: Little Edie Beale's Life After Grey Gardens." **A four-day weekend at a friend's lake house.** An energetic church choir. Book-matched marble. That 1975 Helmut Newton photo *16th Arrondissement, Paris.* Someone who says, "I'm not going anywhere." Someone who says, **"You pick the movie."** Someone who says, **"Let me know how I can help."** The fact that twenty-two of Savannah's twenty-four original town squares still exist. That 2019 Jordan Casteel painting *Serwaa and Amoakohene.* A crisp ten-dollar bill. The fact that a spider has eight eyes. The entire score of *Les Misérables.*

Happy-making things in a difficult world:
That incredible September 4, 2020, *New Yorker* story by Laurie Gwen Shapiro, "The Improbable Journey of Dorothy Parker's Ashes." **That moment the dog goes nuts after being let off the leash.** The freedom of a breezy Saturday afternoon after the house is cleaned and the laundry is done. Clark Terry's recording of "Out of Nowhere." **Supporting your local NPR and PBS stations.** The morning of the baby's due date. The morning of the family reunion. That 1982 David Wojnarowicz painting *Untitled (Burning House).* **Buying a book solely because of its jacket.** Eating a ridiculous amount of Cheetos jumbo puffs with the residue covering your fingertips. "Louis, I think this is the beginning of a beautiful friendship." Schönbrunn Palace. Kensington Palace. Christiansborg Palace. *Cannonball Adderley's Fiddler on the Roof.* **Climbing into the hay loft in the barn.** That 1873 Timothy H. O'Sullivan photo *Ancient Ruins in the Cañon de Chelle.*

The morning of the wedding day.

Things You Might
Consider Doing Today

Carve a watermelon into a basket with scalloped edges and fill with other sliced fruit. Clean out the gutters. Organize the garage. Reroll the outdoor hose into a perfect O. Master the "Single Ladies" dance. Subscribe to NASA's *Houston We Have a Podcast*. Watch *Adam's Rib*. Read that November 29, 2019, *New Yorker* article "The Life Lessons of 'Little Lulu'" by Margaret Atwood. **Try a different cheese on your burger.** Make Chrissy Teigen's banana Bundt bread. **Make a bonfire.** Make a wish. Research your genealogy. Look at that 1961 Slim Aarons photo *Between Sea and Sky*. Shake out and turn the rugs. Organize your thoughts. Get up later tomorrow. **Start reading that author you've always meant to read.** Blast Joe Cocker's recording of "With a Little Help from My Friends." Watch that *Friends* episode "The One with the Embryos" (season 4, episode 12). Call three friends and ask, "What's the funniest thing that happened to you this week?" Watch the video of Michael Phelps breaking the gold medal record at the 2008 Olympics. Chase a dream. **Chase the kids around the yard.** Throw a Frisbee. Find a superhero cape pattern, sew it, and wear it. Google image search "sunset in Kenya." Ask yourself what brings you meaning. Then take a deep breath. And then rinse and repeat after me:

"I will make this day count."

Good thoughts.

Good times.

Good news.

Fall

There's a moment toward the end of summer when the light shifts and the slant and shadows are different. A small but noticeable change that portends a larger one. The days aren't as long as they used to be; plants give up and go to seed; the temperature blissfully drops; the night sky arrives earlier.

It's the beginning of my favorite time of year: fall.

Summer can blaze in its full frenetic glory, but it's the quiet of fall that speaks to me. Give me a chilly day that requires a jacket; a morning in which you see your breath; and a cluster of mums on a front porch.

Give me sweater weather. Football. Cider. Pumpkin picking. Tricks or treats. Multiple viewings of *When Harry Met Sally*. The inevitable slide to the holidays after Halloween. I can pretty much recite *It's the Great Pumpkin, Charlie Brown* from memory. ("I got a rock.")

Yet fall also has a touch of melancholy. It's a transitional time and can stir up memories and buried thoughts. I have a list of a few (very) serious regrets in my life, and some occurred in the fall of a year long ago or in the not-too-distant past. But I've come to believe that like anger, regret is best used as education or motivation. So much change happens in the fall—new school year, quick-dropping temperatures—that it's a good time for reflection, and allows me to make peace with some of those regrets.

It's said that a leaf changes its color a week after the chlorophyll starts to dissipate. A silent, pivotal change has begun. A new season has arrived. Winter may lie ahead in wait, but it's the autumn that causes reflection—and transformation.

Happy-making things in a difficult world:
Symmetrical hay bales in a field that from a distance look like giant pastries. **Not-yet-opened iris buds** that look like closed lobster claws. Old-fashioned gated Otis elevators. Hate-watching [insert reality-TV show]. That feeling right after you finish brushing your teeth. Ida B. Wells, national treasure. Gail Collins, national treasure. Russell Baker, national treasure. Alicia Keys's recording of "Fallin'." **A great song that comes on the radio** when you're stuck in traffic. Good neighbors. That story of how Nora Ephron, while married to Carl Bernstein, correctly guessed the identity of Deep Throat. That Julia Child quote "I enjoy cooking with wine. Sometimes I even put it in the food." **Sitting at the kid's table at a family holiday.** The dessert table at a church potluck. Wayne Thiebaud's cake paintings. A bouquet of sunflowers. Weezer's recording of "Island in the Sun." When you don't want to be the first one to hang up. Someone who says, **"I can't wait to see you!"** Someone who says, "Let's talk." The 2009 New Orleans Saints. The Garden District. Tipitina's. Fiona and Cordelia and Zoe and Myrtle and Kyle and Madison and Misty Day and Delphine. "Sparkling or still?"

Happy-making things in a difficult world:
Looking at Monday as a fresh start. The Crock-Pot. Hanging the new wallpaper correctly. The sound of **waves crashing on the shore** during a night walk on the beach. The quiet part of the woods. **Saltbox houses.** The novels of Elizabeth Strout. The English Beat's recording of "Save It for Later." **French braids. French toast.** French bulldogs. Someone who says, "It's no big deal." Someone who says, "Don't skip a thing—tell me the whole story." Lawrence Welk and Norma Zimmer and Joe Feeney and Myron Floren and Dick Dale and Mary Lou Metzger and Bobby and Cissy and The Lennon Sisters. **Still knowing all the words to your high school cheers.** *SNL*'s "The Perfect Cheer." Candy stripers. Candy canes. Unlikely duos. Betta fish. *Interview* **magazine (the Warhol years).** Dorothy Height, national treasure. Alice Waters, national treasure. Natasha Katz, national treasure. Jennifer Holland's nonfiction *Unlikely Friendships*. That story of the unlikely friendship between Ross Macdonald and Eudora Welty, highlighted in the nonfiction *Meanwhile There Are Letters*. **Pushing through the pain,** literally or figuratively. Pushing through the tough times. That moment when everyone has left the party and it's just before you start cleaning up. Tom Wolfe's white suit.

Mowing the lawn on a diagonal. Street graffiti
that expresses love for someone. Mahalia Jackson's recording of "His
Eye Is on the Sparrow." The Brooklyn Dodgers. The *Fearless Girl* statue.
Your favorite restaurant. Your favorite movie. Your favorite memory.

MIXTAPE:
Songs for a Slow Dance

A slow dance usually happens at a big celebration. Homecoming. A family wedding. An anniversary party. Prom. That moment that the lights dim, the crowd hushes, and people begin to sway. Here are twenty songs to savor the moment. Have a dance with someone you love (and this can also be done at home—you don't have to wait for something special).

"This Time the Dream's on Me" –Annie Ross and the Gerry Mulligan Quartet

"More Than Words" –Extreme

"Sleepy Man" –Patti LuPone

"O-o-h Child" (remastered) –Nina Simone

"The Best Is Yet to Come" –Lorez Alexandria

"Wonderful Tonight" –Eric Clapton

"I Shall Believe" –Sheryl Crow

"(Sittin' on) the Dock of the Bay" –Otis Redding

"If You Were Here" –Thompson Twins

"Lover" (remix) –Taylor Swift and Shawn Mendes

"Baby, I Love Your Way" –Peter Frampton

"When You Say Nothing at All" –Alison Krauss and Union Station

"Breaking Us in Two" –Joe Jackson

"A Case of You" –k.d. lang

"I'd Rather It Was You" –Carly Simon

"You Don't Know Me" –Ray Charles

"Bridge Over Troubled Water" –Linda Eder

"Dream a Little Dream" –Pink Martini and the von Trapps

"True Colors" –Eva Cassidy

"Harvest Moon" –Neil Young

SPECIAL EDITION

Halloween

Happy-making things in a difficult world:

The hum of the neighborhood trick-or-treaters. Sheb Wooley's recording of "Purple People Eater." **Superhero costumes worn by toddlers.** Mike, Dustin, Lucas, and Will dressed up as the *Ghostbusters*. Ichabod Crane's late-night ride home. The Georgetown *Exorcist* stairs. **Bobby Pickett's recording of "Monster Mash."** David S. Pumpkins. Toasting pumpkin seeds. "Double, double, toil and trouble." **Mini-pumpkins and gourds on the steps.** The "Halloween Heist" episodes of *Brooklyn Nine-Nine*. The "Treehouse of Horror" episodes of *The Simpsons*. The "Halloween Surprise" episode of *Parks and Recreation* (season 5, episode 5). Salem. Springwood. The Overlook Hotel. The Bates Motel. *Scary Stories to Tell in the Dark* by Alvin Schwartz. Laurie Strode. Disneyland's "Haunted Mansion." Plastic jack-o'-lantern candy pails. **Mini candy bars. Counting out the candy.** Mussorgsky's "Night on Bald Mountain." Daytime trick-or-treating for the little ones. **A full moon.** Casper. Slimer. Oogie Boogie.

Happy-making things in a difficult world:

A gaggle of honking geese flying north in a V formation. Someone who says, "I've been thinking about you." Someone who says, "Let's catch up." Someone who says, "It's all going to be okay." Djokovic versus Nadal. **The Subway Series.** White subway tiles in a kitchen backsplash. The UK version of *The Office.* Hasbro's Potato Head. **A bucket full of Lincoln Logs.** Old-timey names such as Cecil, Agnes, Myrtle, Walter, and Millicent. The Hollies' recording of "The Air That I Breathe." Billie Jean King, national treasure. Bette Davis, national treasure. Bob Gibson, national treasure. A Lionel train set circling the base of the Christmas tree. Baby goats. Baby ducks. Baby koalas. Copland's "Appalachian Spring." Shaking the Polaroid photo to help it develop faster. **Positive feedback. Negative test results.** Gray days that inexplicably become sunny days. That 1957 photo of Sophia Loren giving Jayne Mansfield side-eye. Red geraniums in the wild. Drinking an ice-cold Coke from a sweaty glass bottle. The Louisa May Alcott House in Concord, Massachusetts. **Really good French onion soup.** People-watching in a doctor's waiting room or on the subway. **"Stand clear of the closing doors!"** The perspective of been there, done that. Scooping the guts and seeds out of a soon-to-be jack-o'-lantern. The beauty of the quilts of Gee's Bend. Supertramp's recording of "Goodbye Stranger." That spot in the road where you know you are almost home.

The care with which a bookseller
selects a staff recommendation.

An attentive but not too attentive waiter.

Mark and Doug and Susan and
Carter and Benton and Carol.

The slam of a wooden screen door.

The aesthetic of Nancy Meyers.

The harmonica solo in the opening
chords of Billy Joel's "Piano Man."

Happy-making things in a difficult world:
Velveeta shells and cheese. That Hiroyuki Nishimura sculpture *Fragile Structure #16*. Christine and Matthew and Richard and New Christine and Richie and Marly and Lindsay and Barb. The Dave Brubeck Quartet's recording of "Someday My Prince Will Come." **The realization that the decade you grew up in has become retro for a new generation.** A 1955 red-and-white Corvette Stingray. That 1955 Phil Stern photo *James Dean in Sweater*. That 1955 René Magritte painting *The Mysteries of the Horizon*. **Ripping open the presents.** Charles Busch's *The Tale of the Allergist's Wife*. The fact that a court reporter must be able to accurately type up to 225 words per minute. Beyoncé's recording of "Irreplaceable." A full bicycle basket. An empty nest. The moment after you replace the ink cartridge. The 29,029 feet that make up Mount Everest. Ordinary miracles. The Vince Guaraldi Trio's recording of "Cast Your Fate to the Wind." The trust of a three-year-old. The exuberance of a new divorcée. The even-keelness of an elder.

Floor seats at an NBA or WNBA game.

Happy-making things in a difficult world:

Bright green buds on the trees. Rosie the Riveter. That April 13, 2020, heartbreakingly beautiful and moving *New York Times* column by Margaret Renkl, "The Clarity That Comes with Hard Times." High school band fundraisers. The National Spelling Bee. Meredith Willson, national treasure. Maya Lin, national treasure. Wilma Mankiller, national treasure. A sixty-four-degree day. On Cloud tennis shoes. Using British slang words, such as *trainers, lift, collywobbles,* and *knackered*. A new color of nail polish. Savoring the last few pages of a book you adore. The ding of the egg timer. Hot dogs at the ballpark. Old, faded red barns. The Supremes' recording of "My Favorite Things." **Pulling the number tab for the deli-counter line and finding it in your coat pocket days later.** Lockets. The print version of the *OED* that comes with a magnifying glass. That photo of Einstein sticking out his tongue on his birthday in 1951. Terrible family photos. **Johnny and Moira and David and Patrick and Alexis and Ted and Stevie and Twyla and Jocelyn and Roland and Bob and Ronnie and Ray.** Erasure's recording of "Blue Savannah." The 1991–1993 Chicago Bulls. Crepe paper streamers festooning the school gym at a dance. The friendship of Carl Reiner and Mel Brooks. Little Free Libraries. Coveralls. Ball jars filled with the bounty of summer. *Talladega Nights*. The sound of a train whistle, early in the morning or late at night. Rolltop desks. The Tiny Kitchen Instagram. Advice from your elders, which 99 percent of the time should be heeded. Jim Lahey's no-knead bread recipe. The fact that Arthur Miller wrote the first act of *Death of a Salesman* in a day. People who help other people.

Graduation

Happy-making things in a difficult world:

That moment you capture your cap after you toss it in the air. **Decorating your cap** so that your family can easily spot you in the crowd. Keeping your tassel. Your family and friends cheering for you as you reach for your diploma. Your class photo. **Your best friend in high school.** Your college roommate(s). Posing for a photo with your favorite teacher. Cleaning out your locker. Cleaning out your dorm room. Someone giving you a [insert school] T-shirt. Someone giving you a "Class of [insert year]" T-shirt from your prospective college. The day you get to stop using, and turn, in your textbooks. Knowing that after this day, your life is going to change forever. **"There is a great future in plastics."** The summer stretching wide open before you. A summer internship to look forward to. A summer job that years from now will remain halcyon and preserved as a great time in your life. *Say Anything.* The after-party, during which you tell someone something you've always wanted to say. Green Day's recording of "Good Riddance." The arrival of **your senior yearbook.** An unforgettable commencement speech. An inspiring valedictorian. Your boring principal. Finally realizing what "bittersweet" feels like. A gym buzzing with energy before the big event starts. **"Pomp and Circumstance."** The optimism of a high school or college senior. Cake. And because it bears repeating: Lin-Manuel Miranda (and his unforgettable 2015 Wesleyan commencement speech).

Things You Might Consider Doing Today

Eat breakfast outdoors. Read that December 22, 1941, Shirley Jackson essay from *The New Republic*, "My Life with R. H. Macy." Motivate yourself to take that one big or small regret that has been clinging to your collar and throw it out the window. Listen to Ella Fitzgerald and Louis Armstrong's 1956 album, *Ella and Louis*. **Clean behind the refrigerator.** Watch a Christopher Guest movie. Read that March 3, 2017, *New York Times* essay by Amy Krouse Rosenthal, "You May Want to Marry My Husband." Change the bathroom soap. Google image search "Badlands National Park + sunrise." Look at the photographs in Carrie Mae Weems's 1990 *The Kitchen Table Series*. Listen to that November 21, 2016, *Fresh Air* interview with Zadie Smith. **Use a new pen.** Watch Ali Stroker's 2019 Tony Award acceptance speech on YouTube. **Remember that who you were doesn't necessarily have to be the person you are now.** Remember that Billie Jean King quote "Champions keep playing until they get it right." Listen to that May 5, 2003, *Morning Edition* interview with Caroll Spinney, "A Life Inside Big Bird." Stop trying to put a square peg into a round hole. Look at the Kehinde Wiley exhibition *The Yellow Wallpaper*. Purchase a toy you once loved but have since lost. Watch that January 12, 2020, *CBS Sunday Morning* segment "Untangling the Mysteries of the Octopus." **Rearrange the living room furniture.** Blast Aretha Franklin's recording of "Eleanor Rigby." If you are lucky enough to be able to do so, ask your grandparents about their first date. Watch the last nine minutes and two seconds of *It's a Wonderful Life*. Hug your kids a little tighter. Hug your pet a little tighter. Hug yourself a little tighter. And then rinse and repeat after me: "What I do matters."

Putting the
last piece
of the jigsaw
puzzle into
place.

Teachers

She drove a baby-blue Porsche (in our small town in the mid-1980s, this was rare). She read S. E. Hinton out loud to us (we reconnected years later when I sent her a signed copy of *The Outsiders*). She traveled the world and once drove ten thousand miles roundtrip from home to Alaska in her *other* sports car. The first time that someone outside of your family or group of friends believes in you is a big deal, and English teacher extraordinaire Mrs. Bullard gave that gift to me in the sixth grade. I was in her homeroom and English class in 1985, and she changed my life.

A great teacher is someone who opens the door for you—sometimes it's just a crack, other times it's wide open with a wave forward. "You should read this because I think you would like it," they might say as they hand you a book that's new to you. "Tell me more," they might ask during a discussion, allowing you to develop and express your own opinion. "You can go there someday too!" they might say when they're talking about a trip that seems impossibly out of reach to you. A great teacher is someone outside your orbit of family and friends who pushes you in new directions. Someone who presents options alongside opportunity. Mrs. Bullard charted the beginning of my course to a fuller version of me.

Think about it. All those red marks on a paper with suggestions in the margin. Yes, each slash stung, but it was growth. Getting into trouble and having to clap the erasers after school both righted a wrong and built character. The coach putting you back in the game showed the power of a second chance. The band director who made you replay the same section over and over until it was perfect demonstrated the value of discipline. The steadying presence of the school janitor who kept the engine of the school running quietly taught you the hard work of dedication.

Your life is full of teachers, if you're lucky. Someone who taught you how to sail. Someone who taught you how to act with grace. Someone who taught you how to pitch. Someone who taught you how to sew. Someone who taught you how to make a perfect biscuit. Someone who taught you how to drive a stick shift. Someone who changes your life. Pat Bullard changed mine.

What teacher—or teachers—changed your world? Have you been a teacher for someone else in your own life?

Happy-making things in a difficult world:
The Conoid Chair from George Nakashima Woodworkers. That
September 26, 2011, Annals of Medicine column in *The New Yorker*
by Atul Gawande, "Personal Best: Top Athletes and Singers Have
Coaches. Should You?" Walking around downtown **Saratoga
Springs, New York.** Walking around downtown
Portsmouth, New Hampshire. Walking around
downtown **Saint Charles, Missouri.** Holsteins dotting
the pasture. Leslie Odom Jr.'s recording of "Standards." Ruth and Nate
and Brenda and David and Keith and Claire and Rico and Vanessa
and Billy and George. Sia's recording of "Breathe Me." **The
Amtrak Café Car. The Amtrak Quiet
Car.** Greta Gerwig, national treasure. Hilary Knight, national
treasure. Julian Bond, national treasure. Vladimir Horowitz's entire
record *Horowitz in Moscow*. The sound quality in a
new pair of headphones. Bass-O-Matic. That 1979
Nancy R. Schiff photo *Seated Portrait of Actor and Comedian Gilda
Radner (1946–1989) Sitting and Propping Her Chin on Her Hand with
Her Arm Resting over Her Leg*. The fact that a football field is 100 yards
long and 53 1/3 yards wide. That 1935 Alice Neel painting *Pat Whalen*.
Drum corps. Bugle corps.

Happy-making things in a difficult world:
A bowl full of ripe red apples. Scanning the microfiche and finding what you were looking for. Putting a pencil behind your ear for safekeeping. Garlic braids. **A whiff of cologne or perfume that reminds you of someone.** A freshly mopped school gym. The dwindling number of miles to go as you near your destination. Sue the Dinosaur. The glide of a new razor. Barbara Morris's 2017 *Washington Post* letter to the editor, "The Kennedy Center's JFK Bust Almost Ended Up at the Bottom of the Atlantic." **The Zion National Park daily sunset livestream.** The entire *MTV Unplugged: Tony Bennett* album, but specifically his rendition of "Moonglow." Coloring inside the lines. That moment at a wedding reception when everyone starts tapping their glasses to get the bride and groom to kiss. Rick and Ilsa. Jane and Renato. Nemo and Dory. Jodie Foster, national treasure. Beverly Cleary, national treasure. The Tuskegee Airmen, national treasures. **Klickitat Street.** Robert Indiana's *Hope* sculpture. **Slow dancing in the kitchen while you cook together.** Stopping at the yellow light just to be safe. The lyrics to Coldplay's "Yellow." The thirteenth-century soaring stained-glass windows of Sainte-Chapelle in Paris. The "throwed" rolls at Lambert's Cafe in Sikeston, Missouri. Those little jelly packets at the diner. Perfect parallel parking.

Happy-making things in a difficult world:

The satisfying punch of **a Lite-Brite peg.** Emptying the full Connect Four board. Setting up Mouse Trap. The newspaper waiting for you on the doorstep. Drinking the good wine. Doris Day's recording of "Pillow Talk." The hiss of the radiator. **The bubbles in S. Pellegrino.** Giving a kick to the logs. Your grandmother's recipe box. That 2009 "I've Got a Feeling" flash mob on Michigan Avenue that opened Oprah's twenty-fourth season. The lunar rock in the Space Window at Washington's National Cathedral. Gaylord Nelson, national treasure. I. M. Pei, national treasure. Loretta Lynn, national treasure. Magritte's 1928 painting *The Lovers.* **Legal pads. Post-its.** The first day of school. **School book fairs.** Scholastic *Weekly Reader.* A friend helpfully stopping you from doing something you might regret. Getting to take off the rest of the day. Someone who says, "Take a break." A good coach. A spool of bakery string hanging from the ceiling. Marzipan animals. Lionel Richie's recording of "Say You, Say Me." An antique mantelpiece that has a hint of smoke. A tweed sports coat with patches on the elbows. Bernard Waber's picture book *Ira Sleeps Over.*

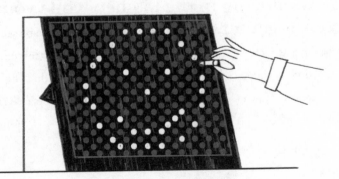

Happy-making things **in a difficult world:**
Sectionals. Sliders. Salad spinners. A weather-beaten Levi's jean jacket that still fits. **A calm bride and groom.** Putting your feet in the backyard kiddie pool on a scorching hot day. Eddie Rabbit's recording of "I Love a Rainy Night." Knowing how to tie a bow tie. **Knowing how to untangle a knot,** figuratively or literally. Depression glass. A complete Fostoria glass punch bowl set. A child's lips stained with Kool-Aid. Norman Lear, national treasure. Sarah Vaughan, national treasure. Grace Brewster Murray Hopper, national treasure. Still remembering your best friend's landline phone number from childhood but not knowing their cell number today because it's programmed into your cell phone and you never actually dial it. A huge slice of Mississippi mud pie. **Getting up early. Being a night owl.** Newport's Cliff Walk. Patsy Cline's recording of "Walkin' After Midnight." Popping the Bubble Wrap. Cracking your knuckles. Snapping your fingers perfectly in time to *The Addams Family* theme song. Selina and Gary and Dan and Jonah and Amy and Mike and Sue and Ben and Kent and Catherine and Marjorie and Richard Splett. **The moment when you know you are in the clear.**

Happy-making things in a difficult world:

A red, white, and blue Lone Star quilt. The Wendy and Emery Reves Collection at the Dallas Museum of Art, which is housed in a replica of their villa. The Platters' recording of "Life Is Just a Bowl of Cherries." **Unreliable narrators.** A protagonist whose morality is tested but not broken. Supporting characters in a novel who become as prominent in your imagination as the protagonist. That family of foxes on that Toronto beach. **A business of ferrets.** The fact that a duck has more than four hundred taste buds. The fact that in 1960 Jane Goodall discovered that chimpanzees could make and use tools. That 1960 Elaine de Kooning painting *Sunday Afternoon.* The Egg Chair by Arne Jacobsen. Requesting a song from Delilah and hearing it on late-night radio. **Marfa, Texas.** The Donald Judd Chair 84. Don Larsen's penultimate pitch in his 1956 perfect game. **The quiet, corner table in the back of the restaurant.** A rowdy group at a table across the restaurant. That April 26, 2020, *New York Times* article by Gabrielle Hamilton, "My Restaurant Was My Life for 20 Years. Does the World Need It Anymore?" The Grand Canyon Skywalk. Someone who says, "Try harder." Someone who says, "Impress me." Shania Twain's recording of "That Don't Impress Me Much." Making the ask. **Helping someone shine their brightest.** Finding your rhythm. A moment of revelation. "Until the day is night and night becomes the day (always)."

Happy-making things **in a difficult world:**
Frosted Flakes. Lucky Charms. Fruity Pebbles. That September 7, 2020, *Guardian* opinion article by Elliot Dallen, "At 31, I Have Just Weeks to Live. Here's What I Want to Pass On." "Wonder Twin powers, activate!" Glass doorknobs. Beth Stern, national treasure. That 2002 Sophie Ryder sculpture *Minotaur with Dog on Shoulder.* That moment after the appetizers arrive. **No line at the post office. No line at the DMV.** No line at the pharmacy. Mariah Carey's recording of "Open Arms." A new canvas on the easel. A dab of Grey Poupon. The fact that orcas must keep one of their eyes open as they sleep. "Where's that piece of paper I had in my hand yesterday morning?" **A crooked smile. A crooked tooth.** Straightening a crooked picture frame. That 1888 Van Gogh painting *Starry Night Over the Rhône.* Tracy and George and Mike and Liz and Seth and Margaret and Dinah and Uncle Willie and C. K. Dexter Haven. A plate of tender buttered asparagus. The moment just before the guests arrive at the party.

Noah Reid's recording of "Simply the Best."

Red Velvet Cake

My grandma was famous for her cooking—she always made extra because you never knew who would conveniently time their visit during supper—but her desserts were the stuff of legend. I once saw her make a peach cobbler from scratch, no recipe required. She knew exactly when a pie should be pulled from an oven, the pivotal moment when the German chocolate cake icing was ready to start to cool, and the precise consistency the dough needed to be in order to produce perfectly fluffed and flaky biscuits for breakfast.

But of all the food she could whip up with seemingly minimal effort—fried chicken crispier than a new sheet of typing paper, tangy spinach salad dazzled with a drizzle of dressing (so that it wasn't goopy), coconut pie with a meringue as high as a pompadour—it's the seven-layer red velvet cake that takes me right back to my childhood and her. You read that correctly: seven.

There's a photo of us together and one of the (many) cakes she made for me is right there in the background. Glass cake plate, dome removed, contents disheveled. In order to make this particularly vertical cake, it required four cake pans of red velvet mix that she would then perfectly halve (with one layer left for scrap eating). She pieced together that cake with the precision of a bricklayer, each level perfectly balanced, no icing smudging the delicate sponge.

A thick wedge of cake is best; you sink your fork into that delicate, thin edge cut from the center first and it gives you just the tiniest of tastes. Red velvet cake is dense and extremely sweet, and best savored smoothly, not scarfed down in a rush. The creamy icing is the perfect counterbalance to the cake, with more than enough sugar to give you a kick in the pants. Sweet and sweeter is the motto of a red velvet cake.

The mixing and baking, the slicing of the layers, the icing making, the assembly of that cake—it was all a lot of work. But that work was an act of love. It irked her that the cakes weren't easily shippable, and I received more than one letter from her that ended with, "If you were here, I would make you a red velvet cake."

What is your favorite dessert? Is there someone who you love or loved that made it especially for you?

That Moment
in Your Life When You . . .
Part 2

Scored the winning run. Provided a lifeline without knowing it. **Had your first kiss.** Had your first beer. Discovered your favorite comedian. Discovered your favorite food. **Turned the corner.** Realized your siblings are people too. Stopped worrying about what other people think. Rolled the dice. Aced the big test. Listened to the whole sermon. Graduated from the kiddie table. **Were responsible for the Thanksgiving turkey.** Jumped in without asking. Signed the lease on your own apartment. Snuck back into the house without your parents knowing. Made your own vegetable stock. Made do with what you had. Made your last student loan payment. Ignored everyone else and listened to your gut. **Started asking for help when you needed it.** Popped the question. Took off the training wheels. Stayed up all night and watched the arrival of dawn. **Did the wrong thing, learned from that bad experience,** and never did that wrong thing again.

Went to your first [insert professional sports team] game. Threw out what you didn't need, literally or figuratively. Started seriously considering which hill to die on and when. **Successfully carried out an entire conversation in a foreign language.** Survived a terrible dinner party. Replaced a propane tank. Changed a flat tire. Bought a nice watch. Caught the bridal bouquet and didn't care. Hit the big 4-0. Closed a door that needed to be closed. Brought the baby home. Nailed the interview. Got the job. Learned that anger is useless except as self-motivation. Understood the value of getting up early.

MIXTAPE:
A Cure for the Mean Reds

The alarm didn't go off when it was supposed to. The coffee got spilled. There was traffic. We've all had those mornings that start off on the wrong foot, so I made you a mixtape to turn that frown upside down. Hope this helps with the terrible, horrible, no good, very bad day.

A	B
"Synchronicity 1" –The Police	"Hey Loretta" –Loretta Lynn
"Spider Pig" –Hans Zimmer (from *The Simpsons Movie: The Music*)	"Hard to Explain" –The Strokes
"Pump It Up" –Elvis Costello & The Attractions	"My Lovin' (You're Never Gonna Get It)" –En Vogue
"I Love It" –Icona Pop and Charli XCX	"Not the Doctor" –Alanis Morissette
"Rolling in the Deep (the Aretha Version)" –Aretha Franklin	"Little Bird (Tee's Alternative Mix)" –Annie Lennox
"Stop!" –Erasure	"Twist and Shout" –The Beatles
"Everybody's Girl" –Debra Monk	"The Sign" –Ace of Base
"Lonely Night (Angel Face)" –Captain & Tennille	"The Long Way Around" –The Chicks
"For Once in My Life" –Stevie Wonder	"Opening: I Can't Turn You Loose" (live) –The Blues Brothers
"The Promise" –When in Rome	
"Cell Block Tango" –*Chicago* (1996 Broadway Cast Recording)	

Things You Might Consider Doing Today

Watch that CNN video of Anderson Cooper talking about the birth of his son. Open up your dictionary at random and memorize the exact meaning of the first word you land upon. **Throw around the football.** Listen to Leslie Odom Jr.'s recording of "Edelweiss." Make Ina Garten's carrot cake with mascarpone frosting. Eat as much dessert as you want. **Stretch for a very long time.** Agree upon a time and a single song with your family or friends and just dance together for a blissful few minutes in person or via Zoom. Listen to Jeff Buckley's 1994 recording of "Hallelujah." Make up your face as if you were Ziggy Stardust. Think about adopting or fostering a pet if you don't have one. Dig up that *60 Minutes* story from 2016 on the construction of La Sagrada Família. Make an origami swan. Look at that 1960 Eliot Elisofon photo of Gloria Swanson standing in the ruins of the Roxy Theater. Read Joan Didion's 1961 essay "On Self-Respect." Watch the ESPN documentary *The Last Dance*. **Change the sheets on the bed.** Change your ringtone. Use the fancy china. Wash the windows. **Pop the cork on some champagne.** Make a stained-glass window out of chalk and tape on the driveway. Watch Neil Simon's *Murder by Death*. Give someone hope. Give someone your time. Give someone your support. Google "Peabody Hotel ducks" and watch the videos (you're welcome). Think about five good things that happened today. Start a journal. Then take a deep breath. And then rinse and repeat after me:

"I can find comfort in the little things."

Winning at the tricky tray, benefit auction, or school raffle.

Happy-making things in a difficult world:

A pair of swans gliding on a still lake. Giant lily pads floating on a pond. Leaves swirling about on a swiftly moving stream. **Steam rising off an outdoor hot tub in a winter setting.** Collective Soul's recording of "The World I Know." McEnroe versus Connors. Seles versus Sabatini. Sampras versus Agassi. The Andrews Sisters. **Zoot suits. Fishnet stockings.** 1940s "Donna" shoes. *The CBS Radio Mystery Theater.* The Book of Kells at Trinity College in Dublin. **The Napoleon III Apartments at the Louvre.** The "Duomo @ 360 degrees" virtual tour. That 1967 Mary Ellen Mark photo *Girl Jumping Over a Wall, Central Park, New York.* **An Aperol Spritz. A Cosmopolitan. Cocktails on the patio at sunset.** Grilling an apple pie on the barbecue. Kids shrieking on the backyard Slip 'n Slide one yard over. Sheryl Crow's recording of "Every Day Is a Winding Road." Ted and Robin and Marshall and Lily and Barney and Tracy and Slapsgiving. **Fountain pens. Ink blotters.** The soothing lilt of Bob Ross's voice. That 1943 Thomas Hart Benton lithograph *Spring Tryout.* Spring training. Summer vacation. Fall bounty. Winter sunrise. Someone who says, "What should we do today?" Someone who says, "What should we do tomorrow?"

Happy-making things in a difficult world:

A stroll through the park at dusk, just as the crickets start to hum. Walking through the garden rows. The fact that Mel Blanc's tombstone says "That's All Folks." Long-form journalism. *The Atlantic. The New Yorker. Time* magazine. Chet Baker's recording of "Embraceable You." Multnomah Falls. Kent Falls. Iguazu Falls. Cormac McCarthy, national treasure. Carol Shields, national treasure. Terry McMillan, national treasure. **That moment when the dinosaur falls apart in *Bringing Up Baby*.** "Remind me to tell you about the time I looked into the heart of an artichoke." That 1977 David Hume Kennerly photo of Betty Ford dancing on the Cabinet Room table. That 1999 Larry Fink photo of George Plimpton. Michelangelo's *Pietà*. Patti LaBelle's recording of "If You Asked Me To." Patti LaBelle's recipe for sweet potato pie. **Hitting the mark. Punching the clock. Embracing the inevitable.** Putting on your pajamas after doing a drive-by at a party that you didn't want to attend but had to attend. Giacometti's 1950 sculpture *Dog*. Seeing the Griffith Observatory floating in the hills on **a clear Los Angeles morning.** Hopeful stories on the evening news. A fully stocked bar cart. New pot holders without scorch marks. **Good olive oil.** Someone who says, "I'm thrilled for you!" Someone who says, "You have it in you to do this." Someone who says, "Don't doubt yourself." Moxie.

Happy-making things in a difficult world:

Curly fries. A forward path. Seatmates on the commuter train that you never speak to but give a morning nod to each day as you approach your regular spot. The rugelach from Zabar's. **Fuzzy caterpillars.** That 1897 Camille Pissarro painting *Boulevard Montmartre, Morning, Cloudy Weather.* **The architecture of a coiled fern fiddlehead.** Frank Gehry's Walt Disney Concert Hall. Zaha Hadid's Guangzhou Opera House. Carla Hayden, national treasure. Marin Alsop, national treasure. Larry Kramer, national treasure. The fact that the style of music is the determining factor differentiating a violin from a fiddle. The entire score of *Fiddler on the Roof.* William the Hippopotamus. The *Free to Be . . . You and Me* recording of "William Wants a Doll." That 1975 photo of Vincent Price with the raven at the Edgar Allan Poe Museum in Richmond, Virginia. **An unkindness of ravens.** "Oh, I'm sorry. Do you have some prior commitment? Some hideous skirt convention you have to go to?" Dinah Washington's recording of "What a Diff'rence a Day Makes!" Weebles. Chia Pets. Pet Rocks. Emily St. John Mandel's novel *Station Eleven.* Hank Aaron's 715th home run. **Finding a four-leaf clover.** Someone who says, "Keep going." Someone who says, "I know I'm in good hands." Someone who says, "Your faith in something may be tested, but hold firm if you believe."

Happy-making things in a difficult world:

Mansard roofs. A really good bowl of matzo ball soup. The perseverance of a small-business owner. Old cash registers whose bells still work. The daily change of the Google icon and the story behind it. Upstairs at Zabar's. Sitting in the "Sally" seat at Katz's Deli. Balcony seats (center) at Carnegie Hall's Stern Auditorium. The chess players in Washington Square Park. Ray-Bans. Ray and Debra and Amy and Robert and Marie and Frank. **Thriving potted plants.** Chocolate Easter bunnies with their ears bitten off. Jeep Wagoneers. Leonard Bast's overnight walk in Forster's *Howards End*. **Searching the night sky to find Orion.** A pair of worn Converse Chuck Taylor high-tops (red, in memory of Bob Minzesheimer, book critic extraordinaire). **Your local pizza place.** Barry Moser's *Wizard of Oz* woodcuts. **Cats who find their spots of sunshine.** Mavis Staples and Jeff Tweedy's recording of "You Are Not Alone." Letters of recommendation. Letters of support. Letters you saved because they were special. Cheryl Strayed's podcast, *Sugar Calling*. The novels of Celeste Ng, but particularly her vivid creation of Mia's photo series of the inside-out stuffed animals in *Little Fires Everywhere*. **Bonfires. Campfires. Freshly toasted s'mores.** That Banksy painting that shredded itself at the auction. The painted quilts of Faith Ringgold. How excited you got as a child when you had the opportunity to sleep in a tent. **Donkey Kong. Frogger. Pac-Man. Ms. Pac-Man.** The bouncy joy of John Denver's recording of "Grandma's Feather Bed." A chocolate shake in a vintage malt glass. **Bendy straws.** A walk on the Freedom Trail in Boston's North End. *The Town*. Ben and Matt. Magnolias in bloom. "Shelby has been driving nails up her arm." Public Image Ltd.'s recording of "Rise." **The act of treading water.**

Happy-making things in a difficult world:

That moment when the photographer asks you all to say, "Cheese!"
That moment when you pull the last clothespin off the clothesline.
That moment when you know you are finally "done." Baby photos of your great-grandparents. Sara Bareilles's recording of "Love Song." That first hour after the power goes out and the house is **lit by candlelight**. Reading your daily horoscope. Opening a tipped-over stack of mail. That 1936 Man Ray painting *Observatory Time: The Lovers*. Bette Midler, national treasure. Kenya Barris, national treasure. Daniel Inouye, national treasure. The fact that the **International Space Station** circles Earth in approximately ninety minutes. The old afghan on the back of the couch. **Lispenard Street.** Tallis House. Hampden College. The fact that a rhinoceros can run at speeds of up to forty miles per hour. J.R. and Sue Ellen and Bobby and Pam and Miss Ellie and Jock and Lucy and Ray and Cliff. That 1928 Tarsila do Amaral painting *A Lua (The Moon)*. Limoges snuffboxes.

The tasseled, tattered bookmark from your childhood.

Winter

The slice of the ice as you skate across the rink. A bowl of spicy chili that burns the tongue. A steaming mug of hot chocolate that melts the mini-marshmallows to form a fluffy, floating dock on top. A scarf that you tuck into the front of your coat for an extra layer of warmth. A wind tunnel that pummels you as you turn a corner.

Winter may be a fallow season of hibernation, but it's also a time for preparation. There are seed catalogs to go through. Vacations to be researched and planned. Snowmen to be built. Walks to be shoveled. Fires to be tended.

With the short days and long nights, hunkering down at home becomes a necessary way of life. Comfort food rules the kitchen. Heavy blankets weigh down the bed. The lamps come on earlier and there's a hint of wood smoke in the air.

Yes, winter is cold and can be gray and dreary, but it can also be magical. Give me trees covered in a thin layer of ice that gleam like just-washed glass in the sunlight. The act of warming up the car and scraping the windshield free. Give me cardinals in the snow. Experiencing the joy of trekking up the hill and sledding back down.

I also love the quiet that descends with winter, muffling everything around you. The silence as the first snow sputters to an end. An early-morning walk in the blinding sun. Sprinkling salt on the sidewalk alone. The stillness is a welcome recharge, a slowing of the hectic pace of life, and a moment to appreciate the spring to come.

What is your favorite winter activity? Can you remember the best hot chocolate you've ever had?

Things You Might Consider Doing Today

Replace your shower curtain liner. Buy a gift card to your favorite local restaurant and have it mailed to your neighbor. Look at that 1972 Brian Rasic photo of Dizzy Gillespie at the Belgrade Jazz Festival. **Buy a ridiculous hat.** Watch the 1985 Chicago Bears' video of "The Super Bowl Shuffle." Clean the stove top. Listen to episode 8 of *The Paris Review* podcast in which Anna Sale and Stockard Channing re-create Dorothy Parker's 1956 interview in the magazine. **Thin out your wardrobe and make a donation pile.** Write a letter of gratitude to someone who changed your life for the better. Look at your old yearbooks. Forgive the person in high school who tortured you. Read John Kenney's November 2018 *New Yorker* piece, "Love Poems for Married People," and then buy all of his books from **your favorite bookseller**. Look at that 1976 Jill Krementz photo of E. B. White typing in **his writing shed**. Take a stroll through the Neue Galerie New York via their Instagram. Listen to Judy Garland's 1964 album, *Judy at Carnegie Hall*, in its entirety. Wipe down your baseboards. Clean out your car, including the glove compartment. **Hug a tree.** Read *The Best Christmas Pageant Ever* by Barbara Robinson. Break out a new toothbrush. Walk a bit longer on your daily constitutional. Make Ina Garten's weeknight Bolognese. **Stay up till midnight and welcome the new day.** Think about what you aren't doing but should be doing and go do it. Think of something you did as a child and loved—jumping rope, skateboarding, skipping rocks—and go do it. Move a piece of art in your home to a new spot. Blast Otis Redding's recording of "Try a Little Tenderness." Then take a deep breath. And then rinse and repeat after me:

"I'm going to do my best."

Opening the mailbox and finding a letter among a stack of bills.

——— ☺ ———

Finding a nest full of eggs on a tree branch.

Happy-making things in a difficult world: 1040 Fifth Avenue. Clematis climbing the mailbox post. The smell of marigolds. **Deadheading the day lilies.** That 1972 Joan Brown painting *The Dancers in a City #2.* That story of how in 1955 **Marilyn Monroe** told the owner of the Mocambo to book her friend Ella Fitzgerald and she would guarantee that the house would be filled with celebrities every night and Ella's show would become **a hot ticket** (she did and it did). That 1961 Eve Arnold photo *Widow Needing Companion. Dora Gribb and Amateur Painter at the Royal Academy of Arts, London.* Mr. Halloween twelve-inch illuminated ceramic nostalgia trees. Westminster Abbey's Poets' Corner. Bryan Stevenson, national treasure. Fran Drescher, national treasure. France Córdova, national treasure. Adam Ant's recording of "Goody Two Shoes." **The first step** onto the hiking trail. The last step of putting the swing set together. Rosie Sayer and Charlie Allnut. Anita and Bernardo. Thad and Patrick. Corky and Violet. Melissa Clark's recipe for blueberry-glazed Bundt cake. The 613 seeds in every pomegranate. The Verve's recording of "Bitter Sweet Symphony." **Telegrams. Anagrams. Bananagrams.**

Happy-making things in a difficult world:

Waffle fries. Pinafores. Petits fours. Purple rhododendron in full bloom. That Iurie Belegurschi photo *Reflection of the Sky*. Two seats at a packed bar that open up directly in front of you just when you're ready to sit. Visiting Haystack Rock in Cannon Beach, Oregon, during **the last moments of sunset.** That 1890–1891 Claude Monet painting *Wheatstacks (End of Summer)*. Neil Young's recording of "Harvest Moon." **A field goal that just barely makes it.** Discovering that the Latin name for *wishbone* is *furcula,* meaning "little fork." The choice you have to make at the fork in the road. Johnny Carson, national treasure. Helen Hardin, national treasure. Jane Wright, national treasure. "Well, nobody's perfect." Gladys Knight and the Pips' recording of "Midnight Train to Georgia." Covent Garden. Tivoli Gardens. **Tuileries Gardens.** Bryan Burrough's February 2016 *Vanity Fair* article, "The Mystery of the Maltese Falcon." Frasier and Niles and Daphne and Martin and Eddie and Roz and Maris. Penny Vincenzi's Spoils of Time trilogy of novels. The ring of the doorbell. **An unexpected package on the doorstep.** The satisfaction upon completion of sweeping the porch. Madeline Kahn's recording of "Getting Married Today." Someone who says, "I'm here for you." Someone who says, "It can be done."

Happy-making things in a difficult world:

Beehive hairdos. Horn-rimmed eyeglasses. Your mother's pearls. B. J. Thomas's recording of "Raindrops Keep Fallin' on My Head." **Being as excited for someone else's good news as if it were your own.** That 2017 *Garden & Gun* article by Julia Reed, "Roll of a Lifetime," which showcases her friendship with Jessica Lange and their road trips through the Mississippi Delta, accompanied by Lange's photographs. **A full day. A clear calendar.** That fresco in the "House of Venus in the Shell" at Pompeii. Rita Moreno, national treasure. Linda Ronstadt, national treasure. Dr. Patricia Bath, national treasure. That nineteenth-century Théodore Rousseau painting *The Forest in Winter at Sunset.* Licking the brownie batter off the mixer beaters. The crinkle of tinfoil. Aluminum pie plates hanging in the garden to scare away critters. Peggy Lee's recording of "Is That All There Is?" The Boston Citgo sign. The maze of Philadelphia's Reading Market. **The fish throwers at Seattle's Pike Place Market.** Callie Khouri's *Thelma & Louise* screenplay. Nadal's win at the 2012 French Open. Someone who says, "Everything will be all right."

That Painting

I've been obsessed with E. L. Konigsburg's 1967 novel, *From the Mixed-Up Files of Mrs. Basil E. Frankweiler*, since I was a kid.

Uncle Dennis sent me a hardcover, which I have to this day. (I was lucky enough to meet Mrs. Konigsburg once at a charity event and have her autograph—picture a looooong line of children, and then tall, twenty-something-year-old me standing at the end waiting to meet her, like a graph that remained static until it spiked at the end.) The thought of two children escaping to the Met, camping out, having free rein of the place at night, and solving a mystery all at the same time was total catnip to me—as a kid and now. The museum is catnip too; you can simply pick a wing and stay there for the day.

One of my favorite paintings is located in gallery 802, the Barbizon School.

Théodore Rousseau's *The Forest in Winter at Sunset* hangs there. Mammoth in scale, approximately five feet high and over eight feet wide, the painting consists of browns, ochre, yellow, and a hint of black. It looks like something out of a fairy-tale fever dream concocted by Tim Burton, but in fact was crafted by Rousseau more than 170 years ago, and, according to the Met, remained unfinished and never exhibited during the artist's lifetime .

In the painting, the Fontainebleau Forest is captured at sunset, a mass of dark limbs and limited sky. The trees reach deep into the heavens with waning yellow sun and dark clouds above, birds (geese?) flying overhead as two peasant figures watch, stopped in their path. The Met says that Rousseau intended to capture the "awe of nature" in the work. To me, the painting is a work of hope.

At first glance it may not seem that way. However, if you look two-thirds to the right of the painting, there is a hint of an opening, the sunset breaking through all of that darkness. The path may be long for our two figures there, but what if home is nearby? Maybe they just wanted to see the sunset. If they are on some sort of journey, maybe the end of that arboreal tunnel is not that far ahead and they will make it through. There's no indication whatsoever that this is the reaction that Rousseau intended. And of course *Forest* may speak to another visitor quite differently, which is another beautiful mystery offered up by the Met.

Think of what the painting has survived in the intervening years since 1867: wars, the Depression, pandemics, millions of visitors. The fact that art can evoke a response from the viewer all these years later is an act of hope.

Do you have a favorite painting? How does it make you feel and why do you love it?

Happy-making things in a difficult world:

A moment of unity. A moment of change. A moment of pride. Wooden butter molds. Butter churns. A pat of butter on top of **a stack of fluffy, warm pancakes.** Mel Tormé's recording of "How Long Has This Been Going On?" The fact that a snail can sleep for three years. Leaning over backward to kiss the Blarney Stone. That Seward Johnson *Unconditional Surrender* statue in San Diego. Holding on to your childhood baseball glove. A beverage that perfectly fits into your car's cup holder. Perfectly symmetrical grocery store displays. **Making plans.** Canceling plans. The theme of your high school prom night. Carly Simon's recording of "Life Is Eternal." **That 1893 Mary Cassatt painting *The Boating Party.*** Dolores Huerta, national treasure. Kareem Abdul-Jabbar, national treasure. Setting your watch five minutes fast. That 1930 Oscar Graubner photo *Margaret Bourke-White atop the Chrysler Building.* **Olaf.** Lumière. **Sebastian.** That moment on *Antiques Roadshow* when the object is revealed to be worth far more than the owner ever expected and they say they will never sell. The exhibit *Boston's Apollo: Thomas McKeller and John Singer Sargent* at the **Isabella Stewart Gardner Museum.** Madison Square Park. Tompkins Square Park. Having a key to Gramercy Park. Dorothy West's novel *The Wedding.* The Sunday comics.

Happy-making things **in a difficult world:**
Teaching a child how to say their name in pig Latin. That particular south-facing spot on Sixth Avenue, around Twelfth Street, where the clock turret of the Jefferson Market Library looks like **the face of an owl**. Icicle Works' recording of "Birds Fly (Whisper to a Scream)." Willy Wonka and Charlie Bucket and Augustus Gloop and Mike Teavee and Violet Beauregarde and Veruca Salt. A "Slam Dunk" bottle of Maker's Mark. The story behind Virginia Schau's 1954 Pulitzer Prize–winning photo, *Rescue on Pit River Bridge*. The Inn of the Five Graces in Santa Fe, New Mexico. **That sound the school bus door makes as it opens and closes.** That moment after you learn the X-ray came back okay. That pop of the soft drink tab as you crack it open. "Do you like scary movies?" The 2,180 miles that make up the Appalachian Trail across fourteen states. Natasha Bedingfield's recording of "Unwritten." Turning on the attic fan on a hot summer night. A surprise that requires a blindfold. **A fold of sheep.** The tight fold of a hospital corner. That 1971 Loïs Mailou Jones painting *Moon Masque*. Turning the page, literally or figuratively.

Steiff
teddy
bears.

Happy-making things in a difficult world:

A moment of clarity. A moment of peace. A moment of hope. The soaring Art Deco lobby of Radio City Music Hall. The giant elevator at Carnegie Hall. The view of Central Park from Jazz at Lincoln Center's Rose Hall. **The complete *Encyclopedia Britannica.*** ELO's recording of "Don't Bring Me Down." The contents of a decades-long untouched hope chest. Thurgood Marshall, national treasure. Eunice Kennedy Shriver, national treasure. Harry Belafonte, national treasure. **A green thumb. A blue sky.** Dolly Parton's cover of "Shine." That 1976 Harry Benson photo of Harper Lee and Truman Capote walking in New York. The annual fifty-thousand-mile migration of the Arctic tern. The Friday cliffhanger on *The Young and the Restless.* The statue of Helen Keller in the National Statuary Hall Collection in the U.S. Capitol. **Post-it notes of encouragement where you least expect them.** That 1970 Alma Thomas painting *The Eclipse.* The fact that engineer Emily Warren Roebling led the construction and completion of **the Brooklyn Bridge** after her husband, the chief engineer, fell ill. The fact that it takes ten to fourteen days for a monarch butterfly to emerge from a chrysalis. Manual typewriters. The public typewriter at Literati Bookstore in Ann Arbor. Alice Hoffman's novel *Illumination Night.* Having to take **a ferry ride** to your vacation destination. And because it bears repeating: Lin-Manuel Miranda (and his book *Gmorning, Gnight!: Little Pep Talks for Me & You,* illustrated by Jonny Sun).

Happy-making things in a difficult world:

That May 26, 2020, profile of ninety-two-year-old Holocaust survivor Marga Griesbach in *The Cut*, "Surviving It All," by Rebecca Traister. The sound of your fingernails on an old washboard. The satisfying snap of a Tupperware lid. Billie Holiday's recording of "What a Little Moonlight Can Do." That moment **when you turn on the light again** after replacing a burned-out light bulb. That 1943 Gordon Parks photo *Woman and Dog in Window, Harlem, New York*. Window shopping. Sandra Cisneros, national treasure. Janet Mock, national treasure. Whoopi Goldberg, national treasure. That moment when the usher gives you your *Playbill*. That moment **when the house lights go down before the concert starts.** Thompson Twins' recording of "If You Were Here." A box of Triscuits. A box of keepsakes. A box of your favorite Girl Scout cookies. That 1960 Lygia Clark sculpture *Critter Bird in Space*. The fact that the bee hummingbird weighs less than a penny. A conspiracy of lemurs. Someone who says, "Tell me all about your day." Someone who says, "Tell me all about your trip." Someone who says, "Tell me the truth." Checking your coat.

Checking out a library book. Benjamin Alire Saenz's novel *Aristotle and Dante Discover the Secrets of the Universe*. Hooper's Store. The Shire. Narnia. **The light at the end of the tunnel.**

Things You Might
Consider Doing Today

Clean the oven. Subscribe to a new magazine. Plant a plant. Plant an intention. Teach your kids the lyrics to They Might Be Giants' recording of "Birdhouse in Your Soul." **Have a second cocktail this evening.** Pick any direction and take a long drive. Reorganize the bookshelves. **Organize your passwords.** Read the Shel Silverstein poem "Falling Up." Listen to the pianist's late-evening set on the Marie's Crisis Facebook page (Maries Group). **Have a big dinner.** Call your college roommate. Check on someone who wouldn't expect you to do so. Help someone who needs help but hasn't asked. Follow the advice of Prince and **jam out to "Let's Go Crazy."** Put on your Halloween costume to take out the garbage. Put up some Christmas lights. Search on YouTube for "Lin-Manuel + Vanessa Wedding Video" to see the greatest wedding surprise ever. Get rid of the bathroom scale. **Take a hot bath by candlelight.** Let go of a grudge. Donate to the North Shore Animal League. Watch all of the *Friends* Thanksgiving episodes. Watch the *Cheers* episode "Thanksgiving Orphans" (season 5, episode 9) and relish that last scene. Bake a Duncan Hines chocolate cake, cover it with vanilla frosting, and then eat two slices. Listen to Otis Redding's recording of "(Sittin' on) the Dock of the Bay." Then **take a deep breath** because there is still so much goodness surrounding you in the world. And then rinse and repeat after me: "*Chart your own course.*"

Spring

There is that moment in spring when the day is warm enough to shed the winter coat for good. Gloves and scarves and toboggans are put away. Buds on the trees begin to pop. Crocus shoot up from the ground. Restaurants open their outdoor seating. Ducklings trot along behind their parents. The world wakes up from a winter slumber as the days start to grow longer.

Spring breaks are taken. Family getaways are planned. Snowbirds return north. The countdown to the last day of school begins. Pastels reappear. Bicycles are brought out of storage, new air pumped into the tires. Seedlings are started in egg cartons. Postgraduation plans are formulated. The sound of lawn mowers permeates the neighborhood. Allergies go crazy.

Spring cleaning starts. Windows are washed. Laundry is hung outside. New welcome mats are put out. Grills are scrubbed. Screens are washed.

My grandma Mimmie always said you had to plant potatoes on Good Friday, the first step in making the garden that would reach its zenith months later. In spring, you're able to plant those potatoes. And that's because spring is a season of hope. Change is in the air.

Do you have a favorite spring-cleaning activity? What was the best spring break trip you ever took?

That
Carrie Fisher
quote

"Take your
broken heart,
make it
into art."

Happy-making things in a difficult world:

The unfurling of a Fruit Roll-Up. Light dappling a trickling stream. Lucchese cowboy boots. A favorite song playing loudly on a neighbor's radio that carries into your yard. The entire score of *The Book of Mormon*. **The moment after the sidewalk is swept.** A set of Smith & Hawken garden tools. Planting the seeds, literally or figuratively. That 1962 Allan D'Arcangelo painting *U.S. Highway 1, Number 5*. A kitchen that has a window with a view over the sink. Houseboats. Tugboats. Your grandmother's clip-on earrings. That 1948–1952 Abbie Rowe photo *Bulldozer in the White House*. Opening the blinds to the morning sun. **Mondo posters. Hatch Show Print.** The books of David Macaulay, particularly *The Way Things Work*. Spiking the volleyball. A hotel bathroom with a claw-foot tub. The authority of someone with a clipboard. Ava DuVernay, national treasure. Diane Sawyer, national treasure. Franklin Chang Díaz, national treasure. **Worry beads.** Keely Smith's recording of "Someone to Watch Over Me." Someone who says, "Rome wasn't built in a day." Someone who says, "No one said it would be easy." Someone who says, "Focus on the positive." The fact that a piano is made up of more than twelve thousand parts. **A seasonal floral arrangement** in a vintage watering can. Passing the dish to the person on your right at the table and taking the next dish from the person on your left. Angela Carter's short-story collection *The Bloody Chamber*.

Happy-making things **in a difficult world:**
An early-evening stroll through an old cemetery. A sunrise walk through the woods. The September 2, 2016, *New York Times* article "Celebrity Answering Service Endures, Its Secrets Intact" by Alex Vadukul. **Watching a funny movie** on a plane and getting side-eye from your seatmates when you burst out laughing into the quiet. Harper Pitt's "Night Flight to San Francisco" monologue from *Angels in America*. Audra McDonald, national treasure. Terrence McNally, national treasure. The Gershwins, national treasures. Howard Jones's recording of "Life in One Day." **Being seated next to the life of the party.** The half-time performance of the high school marching band. Tailgating at a college football game. A stack of new books. A receding stack of dishes as you wash. Zora Neale Hurston's novel *Their Eyes Were Watching God.* The fact that Alice Walker bought a tombstone with the engraving "A Genius of the South" in 1973 for Zora Neale Hurston's unmarked grave, which she discovered. Beck's recording of "Devils Haircut." The fact that Devils Tower in Wyoming was named the United States' first national monument. Sandy and Danny and Rizzo and Kenickie and Frenchy and Jan and Marty and Doody and Sonny and Cha-Cha DiGregorio. **Art as protest. Art as connection.** "Art isn't easy."

MIXTAPE:
Please Pass the Mashed Potatoes

Whether you're eating on TV trays or at the dining room table, scarfing down food while standing over the kitchen counter or grabbing something on the go, take a few moments to savor the day. And here are a few songs to accompany your supper.

"Blue Moon" –Billie Holiday

"The Air That I Breathe" (2008 remaster) –The Hollies

"If Not for You" –Bob Dylan

"He's So Shy" –The Pointer Sisters

"What a Diff'rence a Day Makes" –Dinah Washington

"Dream Kitchen" –Frazier Chorus

"You Never Can Tell" –Chuck Berry

"My One and Only Love" –Art Tatum and Ben Webster

"I Love the Way You're Breaking My Heart" –Rachael & Vilray

"Damn I Wish I Was Your Lover" –Sophie B. Hawkins

"Make Someone Happy" –Jimmy Durante

"Orange Colored Sky" –Natalie Cole

"Girlfriend Is Better" –Talking Heads

"Stars and the Moon" –Audra McDonald

"Love Plus One" –Haircut 100

"She's Got You" –Rhiannon Giddens

"Summer Samba (So Nice)" –Astrud Gilberto

"The Pearl" (remastered) –Judee Sill

"Got to Give It Up (Part 1)" –Marvin Gaye

"Carolina in My Mind" –James Taylor

Happy-making things in a difficult world:

The Yellow Pages. *TV Guide.* A Philco Cathedral radio. That 1976 photo of Jacqueline Kennedy Onassis trying on Empress Alexandra's fur coat at the Pavlovsk Museum in Russia. **Three Pines. St. Mary Mead.** 221B Baker Street. Walk the Moon's recording of "Shut Up and Dance." Antique holiday postcards with indecipherable notes on them. **When the B side of the record becomes a hit.** Dorothy Wickenden's nonfiction *Nothing Daunted: The Unexpected Education of Two Society Girls in the West.* A packed attic filled with undiscovered treasures. **A washer and dryer in the unit.** The Temple of Dendur. The story of how the Frank Lloyd Wright–designed living room from the Francis W. Little house in Wayzata, Minnesota, ended up at the Metropolitan Museum of Art. Paper airplanes zooming across a classroom. Recess. Your high school locker combination. **Sidney Poitier, national treasure. Annie Dodge Wauneka, national treasure.** Rachel Carson, national treasure. The Judds' recording of "Love Can Build a Bridge." Sliding down the banister. Sliding across the freshly mopped wooden floor in your socks. The entire score of *The Secret Garden.*

Happy-making things in a difficult world:

That June 9, 2020, *New York Times* article "Donna Tartt on the Singular Voice, and Pungent Humor, of Charles Portis." Matching and then harmonizing with the pitch of the vacuum cleaner. Crystal Gayle's recording of "Don't It Make My Brown Eyes Blue." **That moment of sweet shock** when you jump into a frigid pool on a sun-soaked, steamy summer afternoon. **Knowing someone who owns a boat.** The Kosta Boda "Fenix" decanter designed by Kjell Engman. Beauford Delaney's 1963 painting *James Baldwin*. Learning that the lovely post-rain smell is called petrichor. The fact that if your second toe is longer than your first toe, it means you have a "Morton's toe." Ordering a Shirley Temple as an adult. **Recliners at the movie theater.** E. L. Konigsburg's novel *Jennifer, Hecate, Macbeth, William McKinley, and Me, Elizabeth*. Allowing yourself to wallow for twenty-four hours. Ralph and Alice and Ed and Trixie. Nina Simone's recording of "My Baby Just Cares for Me." Someone who says, **"Let me take care of that for you."** Someone who says, "Let me know you got home okay." Jelly doughnuts. "Opportunity is not a lengthy visitor."

Happy-making things in a difficult world:
Philately. Cartography. Numismatics. Vecturists. Sophie Gamand's *Wet Dog* portraits. **Snipping the ends of the roses** and cleaning out the vase water each day to **extend the blooms** a bit longer. "525,600 minutes." Horton Foote's screenplay and stage play *The Trip to Bountiful*. Someone who lets you use their shoulder as a pillow. Someone who tickles you to the point of silent laughter. Someone who **tucks you into bed at night.** Liza Minnelli's recording of "Losing My Mind," produced by the Pet Shop Boys. **Alma mater sweatshirts. Alma mater sweatpants.** Alma mater ball caps. Catching the train just before it leaves the station. The Miracles' recording of "You've Really Got a Hold on Me." The twirl of the **barbershop pole.** The twirl of the **villain's mustache.** The twirl of the Hula-Hoop. Barbara Cartland's cotton candy–shaped hair. Adding salt to a hand-cranked ice-cream maker. A bulletin board covered in photos and memorabilia. The time it takes to write a handwritten letter. That 2019 Kathy Butterly sculpture *Crossed Arms*. Christy and Bonnie and Marjorie and Jill and Wendy and Tammy and Adam. Looking through the door's peephole. **Paintball.** Snuggling on the couch.

Happy-making things in a difficult world:

That moment after the ice cream headache stops. That moment the countdown clock begins at 11:59 p.m. on New Year's Eve. The entire score of *Crazy for You*. The fact that you cannot hold your nose and hum at the same time. **That "convention" scene on the pitching mound in *Bull Durham*.** An obstinacy of buffalo. A cauldron of bats. Joseph Lorusso's painting *Times Like These*. **Aloysius.** Paddington. **Corduroy.** The Beautiful South's recording of "A Little Time." The determination of the faithful. The resilience of the experienced. Patricia Wald, national treasure. Katharine Graham, national treasure. Diahann Carroll, national treasure. Someone who says, "Good call." Someone who says, "Tomorrow will be better." **Roller skates.** The Roxy. Ice skates. Wollman Rink. "I read somewhere that everybody on this planet is separated by only six other people. Six degrees of separation. Between

us and everybody else on this planet." Playing "Six Degrees of Kevin Bacon." The first to arrive. The last to leave. Belinda Carlisle's recording of "Mad About You." Writing a secret in the sand and letting the tide sweep it away.

Happy-making things in a difficult world:

Clapping the erasers. Writing "WASH ME" on a grimy car rear window. Thelma Ritter, national treasure. Hanna Holborn Gray, national treasure. Mario Guerra Obledo, national treasure. That June 24, 2020, announcement that "NASA Names Headquarters After 'Hidden Figure' Mary W. Jackson." Someone who says, **"I'm so happy for you!"** Someone who says, **"Wanna grab a bite?"** The Grange. The Morris-Jumel Mansion. That 1979 Cindy Sherman photo *Untitled Film Still #45*. A meticulously curated and as-yet-untouched cheese board. Block parties. A chorus of "Bless you!" after a sneeze. Vanessa Williams's recording of "Save the Best for Last." An unexpected detour that creates a lasting memory. Eleanor and Chidi and Tahani and Jason and Michael and Janet. That 1980 Bernice Bing painting *Burney Falls*. Derek Jeter's career final at-bat in 2014 at Yankee Stadium against the Baltimore Orioles. Caroline Preston's 1997 novel, *Jackie by Josie*. *New Zoo Revue*. *The Letter People*. That March 23, 2015, essay in *The Nation* by Toni Morrison, "No Place for Self-Pity, No Room for Fear." **Rodeo Drive. Regent Street.** Place Vendôme. Art Tatum and Ben Webster's recording of "My One and Only Love." The fact that when bats fly out of a cave, they turn left every time. The entire score of *Bat Boy: The Musical*.

Hanging
the wash on
the clothesline
on a hot, bright
summer morning.

Things You Might Consider Doing Today

Clean out the old shed. Bake the Upgraded German Chocolate Cake recipe from Sally's Baking Addiction. **Cut some flowers from the garden** and give them to your neighbor. Listen to Carol Channing's spoken-word recording of "Housework." Read that February 13, 2000, *New Yorker* piece "Complications" by Wendy Wasserstein. Read that May 27, 2020, *Smithsonian* article "Ancient Roman Mosaic Floor Unearthed Beneath Italian Vineyard." Listen to *Oh, Hello: The P'dcast.* **Start composting. Stop complaining.** Listen to the Pointer Sisters' recording of "He's So Shy." Take an evening drive. Go for a morning bike ride. Watch *Uncle Buck.* Watch *Auntie Mame.* **Wash the curtains. Iron the sheets.** Sleep on the other side of the bed. Google image search "LACMA + lights." Start one of **Denise Mina's crime novels.** Search YouTube for the NBC Sports Films special *More Than Gold: Jesse Owens and the 1936 Berlin Olympics.* Make a donation. Make someone else's day. **Show up. Slow up. Loosen up.** Dance to Marvin Gaye's "Got to Give It Up (Part 1)." Ask yourself what makes you happy. Think about that. Then take a deep breath. And then rinse and repeat after me:

"I can do anything I set my mind to."

An Ode to Hostess

As a kid, some of the weekends I spent with my dad involved working the early shift at his grocery store. I should put "working" in quotes because my shift as a bagger, and later cashier, ended fairly swiftly. There were other things to do, like hide out and take a nap in the back, read every magazine at the register, dive into a paperback from the spinner rack, and grab a small carton of milk and some Hostess treats until we left for the day.

Honey Buns. Fruit Pies. Sno Balls. Suzy Q's. Ho Hos. Zingers. Ding Dongs. Donettes. Twinkies. CupCakes. To this day I can see one in a drugstore, or at a gas station, or in the supermarket, and those early-shift Saturdays at the store come roaring back. I can still feel the sugar rush now.

Filling is key to all of the snacks except the Honey Bun, which was always my least favorite. Honey Buns were too easily smooshed, and the icing had usually melted and stuck to the wrapper, which ripped the bun apart. I wasn't a huge fan of Fruit Pies either, especially if they were cracked or anything other than cherry flavored (the apple chunks were always cut too big). Sno Balls were also a next-to-last choice, as their igloo-shaped shell could harden a bit and the textures never meshed correctly.

On the other hand, Suzy Q's were fun. I liked to separate them—like an Oreo, you had to twist them carefully apart—and eat like two parts of a sandwich. Ho Hos also involved deconstruction: the key was being able to unroll the chocolate topping in as large a piece as possible (like unwrapping a Kraft Single without a single crack) and keeping that layer separate in order to experience two different snacks in one (however, once touched, the thin layer of chocolate melted easily).

Zingers were basically a red, coconut-covered Twinkie that couldn't touch the original in taste. Ding Dongs were always a tricky choice, as they could take on a hard consistency with their outer shells. Donettes were a package of individual treats, but the powdered sugar left too much of a debris trail, a mini-sugar crime scene. Twinkies were the runner-up if a choice was possible: the sponge-to-cream ratio was just right, and they infamously hold their taste and shape forever.

For me, it was always the Hostess CupCake for the win. Perfectly proportioned. A decorative icing scallop on top. Just enough cream filling inside. A spongy consistency that meshed with its hard chocolate topping. The little piece of cardboard underneath to keep the cupcake in place and in form. That small piece of heaven and a small milk, along with the latest *People* magazine, added up to the perfect way to spend a Saturday morning on break at the store.

For those of you who like the Little Debbie snacks, I salute you. However, I cannot join your ranks. Dad once gave my friends and me a case of Oatmeal Creme Pies for our road trip to Biloxi, Mississippi, for spring break our junior year of college. We devoured too many of them during that weeklong trip, and to this day the smell alone sends me back to that feeling, thirty-some-odd years ago, of my stomach unpleasantly full of Oatmeal Pies.

What were your favorite snacks as a kid? When was the last time you had one? Have you ever tried to make them at home?

MIXTAPE:
Quieter Than Study Hall

Sometimes you just need a little peace and quiet. Music can help provide that escape—the perfect background to settle the mind, wind down, or read. I've created a quiet music playlist for you, perfect for an early bird getting the worm, a night owl, or a moment to curl up with a good book.

"The Heart Asks Pleasure First" (*The Piano* soundtrack) –Michael Nyman

"Main Titles" (*The Cider House Rules* soundtrack) –Rachel Portman

"Morning Passages" (*The Hours* soundtrack)" –Philip Glass

"Claire de Lune" (*Ocean's Eleven* soundtrack) –The Philadelphia Orchestra

"Sunday" –Ben Webster and Oscar Peterson

"Cinema Paradiso" –Chris Botti and Yo-Yo Ma

"On Golden Pond (Main Theme)" (*On Golden Pond* soundtrack) –Dave Grusin

"Song to the Moon (Excerpt from the Opera Rusalka)" (*Driving Miss Daisy* soundtrack) –Gabriela Benackova and the Czech Philharmonic Orchestra

"L'Amour Est un Oiseau Rebelle (Habanera)" (*Carmen*, Act 1) –Maria Callas

"Flying over Africa" (*Out of Africa* soundtrack) –John Barry

"Dawn" (*Pride and Prejudice* soundtrack)" –Jean-Yves Thibaudet

"Willoughby" (*Sense and Sensibility* soundtrack) –Patrick Doyle

"(In the) Wee Small Hours (Of the Morning)" –Hazel Scott

Bach Orchestral Suite No. 3 in D Major, BWV 1068 –Lang Lang

Scarlatti Sonata in A Minor, K 59, L241 –Vladimir Horowitz

"La Valse d'Amélie" (*Amélie* soundtrack) –Yann Tierson

"Introduction (Titles)" (*Edward Scissorhands* soundtrack) –Danny Elfman

Bach Cello Suite No. 1 in G Major, BWV 1007 –Pablo Casals

"Il Postino (trio version)" –Luis Bacalov

"Book of Days" –Enya

That Tasha Tudor quote:

"Life isn't long enough to do all you could accomplish. And what a privilege even to be alive. In spite of all the pollutions and horrors, how beautiful this world is. Supposing you only saw the stars once every year. Think what you would think. The wonder of it!"

Happy-making things in a difficult world:

A backyard scavenger hunt. A swinging kitchen door. A tomato, mozzarella, and pesto sandwich. Super Grover. *The Monster at the End of This Book.* Little Golden Books. **Costume parties.** Seeing [insert ridiculous thing] at the store and talking yourself out of buying it and then going back to the store and seeing it again and buying it. *RHONY.* "Jovani!" The fifteen letters that comprise **"Supercalifragilisticexpialidocious."** The six slices that make up the Trivial Pursuit pie. The four nucleotides that make up the two strands of DNA. The Plain White T's recording of "Hey There Delilah." **Each daily rip of the page-a-day calendar.** The chatter in the hair salon. An apartment with a balcony. The Van Cleef & Arpels "Ludo Hexagone" bracelet. Will Shortz, national treasure. Samantha Irby, national treasure. Raúl Julia, national treasure. Mastering the eyelash curler. **The power of the ripple effect.** That 2005 Mario Testino photo *Josh Hartnett.* The view from the Rainbow Room, on the sixty-fifth floor of 30 Rockefeller Center. Being accountable for one's actions. **Pinning on the boutonniere.** The sound of the slide of the minivan door. The smell of lemon zest. Someone who says, "Are you ready?" Someone who says, "You should join us!" Someone who says, "I have no regrets." That 2001 Do-Ho Suh sculpture *Some/One.* The blue-striped *Dear Evan Hansen* shirt. Closing up the cabin for winter. Malcolm Forbes's Fabergé egg collection.

Happy-making things in a difficult world:

That moment after dinner is done but before the table is cleared. That May 29, 2006, Personal History story in *The New Yorker*, "Nora Ephron's Apartment: A Love Story." Extra butter in the freezer. An extra loaf of bread in the freezer. Sarah Vaughan's recording of "That's the Way It Should Be." **Bumper cars. Whac-A-Mole.** Screaming with abandon while on the Scrambler. Beethoven's Piano Sonata No. 8 in C minor, Op. 13. Edna Lewis, national treasure. Janet Rowley, national treasure. Gerda Weissmann Klein, national treasure. DJ Jazzy Jeff & the Fresh Prince's recording of "Summertime." Packing the cooler with a fresh bag of ice. **Funny-shaped ice cubes.** The longest day of the year. The shortest day of the year. Making friends with the people seated next to you at the concert. Someone who says, "I can't use these tickets. Would you like them?" Someone who says, "Use your time wisely." The Drifters' recording of "Under the Boardwalk." The sculptural beauty of worn driftwood on the beach. Coco Dávez's 2019 Faceless portrait series, but particularly her *Richie Tenenbaum* painting. A fully restored Airstream. That story of how in 2007 John Maloof bought a box of negatives for $400 at an auction house, which ultimately led to his discovery and championing of the remarkable photography of Vivian Maier. The entire score of *E.T.* Little League baseball and softball. **A fully expanded Jiffy Pop.**

That June 13, 2020, *New York Times* First Person essay by Amanda McCracken, "Finally, a Wedding. It Was About Time." Trio's recording of "To Know Him Is to Love Him."

Happy-making things in a difficult world:

That moment when the beeping of a truck backing up stops. Learning that the upper part of a pointe shoe worn by ballet dancers is called the "vamp." Sara Lawrence-Lightfoot, national treasure. Margarethe Cammermeyer, national treasure. Rob Reiner, national treasure. **"As you wish."** Madeline Miller's novel *The Song of Achilles*. **That bubbling sound of a percolator.** Canapés. Tears for Fears' recording of "Sowing the Seeds of Love." The promise of a packet of seeds. Dulce Pinzón's photography series *The Real Story of the Superheroes*. **Managing to hold strong when you just want to fall apart.** Julia Child's recipe for beef bourguignon. That 1875 Thomas Eakins painting *The Gross Clinic*. Michael S. Rosenwald's June 24, 2015, *Washington Post* article, "What Novelist Kent Haruf Taught Me about Writing and Life" (you're welcome). Someone who says, **"Should we open another bottle of wine?"** Someone who says, **"You don't need to bring anything."** Someone who says, **"I'll bring dessert."** Nat King Cole's recording of "Straighten Up and Fly Right." The Frick Collection in New York City. The Osage Nation Museum in Pawhuska, Oklahoma. *Match Game*. *Press Your Luck*.

Happy-making things in a difficult world:

The thunderous splat of a water balloon hitting its mark. OMD's recording of "So in Love." Hannah Martin's June 15, 2020, *Architectural Digest* feature, "The Story Behind Henri Matisse's Iconic Woodland Motif." That October 22, 2006, *New Yorker* profile of Suzan-Lori Parks, "The Show-Woman," by Hilton Als. The fact that **Fala** is buried next to **FDR** and **Eleanor.** John Rowell's 2003 short-story collection, *The Music of Your Life.* **Getting the giggles in church.** Patience being rewarded. That 1971 Romare Bearden painting *The Block.* Jill and Sabrina and Kelly and Bosley and Charlie. Sophie B. Hawkins's recording of "As I Lay Me Down." **Getting up early** and **deciding to go back to bed.** The fact that Fairbanks House in Dedham, Massachusetts, is the oldest house in America. Sarah and A. Elizabeth Delany's nonfiction with Amy Hill Hearth, *Having Our Say: The Delany Sisters' First 100 Years.* **Having your needs met. Giving to others.** The moment when the last song begins to play at your first dance. That December 24, 1968, **Bill Anders photo,** *Earthrise.* The fact that a species of fly has the longest animal name on record: *Parastratiosphecomyia sphecomyioides.* The entire score of *Chess.*

Happy-making things in a difficult world:

Personalized M&M's. The art of calligraphy. Accepting a last-minute invitation wholeheartedly. Last call. Judy Collins's recording of "Send in the Clowns." That 2019 John Lewis department store commercial featuring **Edgar the Dragon.** That 2019 Tyler Mitchell photo *Untitled (Group Hula Hoop)*. **Twister. Simon. Uno.** Ted Demme's 1994 film, *The Ref.* That quote from high school basketball coach Tim Notke "Hard work beats talent when talent doesn't work hard." **A long, boozy lunch with old friends.** Round-robin letters. That 2006 Janet Fish painting *Lorna and Jane.* The summer solstice sunrise and sunset livestream from **Stonehenge.** The fact that jousting is the state sport of Maryland. Benjamin Dreyer's nonfiction, *Dreyer's English: An Utterly Correct Guide to Clarity and Style.* Pat Summitt, national treasure. Denzel Washington, national treasure. Echo and the Bunnymen's recording of "The Killing Moon." **A shrewdness of apes. A pandemonium of parrots. A tiding of magpies.**

Happy-making things in a difficult world:
People who still have landlines. People who still write checks. People who still prefer vinyl. Sinatra and Jobim's recording of "Quiet Nights of Quiet Stars." **Nicknames that stick.** Malcolm and Lois and Hal and Francis and Reese and Dewey. Ina Garten's pain perdu recipe from *Barefoot in Paris.* **Snow globes from vacation spots.** Making a snowman. An extra blanket on the bed on a chilly night just when you need it. That 1977 Firooz Zahedi photo of Elizabeth Taylor cooking fried chicken at Atoka Farm. The Clapper. Anthropomorphizing inanimate objects around the house. Dancing to "Y.M.C.A." at the wedding reception with your entire family. That 1932 John Steuart Curry painting *The Flying Codonas.* Someone who says, **"Change is the one constant."** Someone who says, **"Walk it off."** Someone who says, **"Let's hug it out."** Tabasco chipotle hot sauce. Figuratively moving the goalposts. Tongue twisters in general, but specifically "How many Lowe's could Rob Lowe rob if Rob Lowe could rob Lowe's?" The bravery in the attempted use of a neti pot. **Winning the dare.** The morning after the first frost. A car with a sunroof. Vanity license plates. **The Atchison, Topeka and Santa Fe Railway.** R. L. Stine's Goosebumps series. A song that gives you goose bumps. Rebecca Richards-Kortum, national treasure. Nell Carter, national treasure. Gio Benitez, national treasure. Judy Holliday's recording of "The Party's Over."

Happy-making things in a difficult world:
Tomato pincushions. Stevie Nicks's recording of "Stand Back." The
Mystery Spot in Santa Cruz, California. Roswell, New Mexico. The
opening credits of *Soap*. That 2009 John Grisham short story "Funny
Boy." **The endless options within a diner
menu.** Having a deep conversation while waiting to be seated at
your table. Sarah Vaughan's recording of "So Many Stars." Setting up
the **coffee maker** the night before and waking up to a fully
brewed pot the next morning. Lindsay Anderson's 1987 film,
The Whales of August. The fact that whales can navigate by making
clicking sounds. That 2017 William Matthews watercolor *Blue Door*.
Viola Davis, national treasure. Evelyn Dubrow, national treasure. Paul
Monette, national treasure. The fact that books checked out at the
Library of Congress must be read on the premises.
That Stephen Wiltshire 2019 drawing *London Bus at Piccadilly Circus,
London*. The ding of the microwave. Being the second one to hang up.

Things You Might Consider Doing Today

Learn a random phrase in Italian, such as "Buongiorno, vorrei un gelato in coppetta," and use it. Read that November 13, 2019, *New York Times* story by Taffy Brodesser-Akner, "This Tom Hanks Story Will Help You Feel Less Bad." Add a pop of color to the living room via flowers or new throw pillows. **Use the placemats.** Read that Maya Angelou poem "On the Pulse of Morning." Choose a signature cocktail and stick to it. Listen to Christopher Walken's 1997 recording of Poe's "The Raven." Google image search "Rocky Mountains + autumn." Look at that 1989 George Kalinsky photo *Rookie Air: Michael Jordan, Madison Square Garden.* Read that June 2, 2017, *New York Times* Modern Love column by Helen Ellis, "Making a Marriage Magically Tidy." **Repair something that needs to be repaired,** figuratively or literally. Listen to Mary Chapin Carpenter's recording of "Halley Came to Jackson." Scrub the sink. Dust the blinds. Look at that 2010 Roger Shimomura painting *Shimomura Crossing the Delaware.* Watch a little less TV. Take a break from the cell phone or tablet. Buy a Sara Lee classic cheesecake and eat it. Crank Bette Midler's recording of "Beast of Burden." Offer yourself praise. Offer someone help. Offer someone hope. Then take a deep breath. And then rinse and repeat after me:

"It's okay to eat the entire pint of ice cream today."

Taking the Leap

More than twenty-five years ago I graduated from Southern Illinois University (Go Salukis!) on a Friday, partied and packed all weekend, and then, on Monday, with my roommate Casey, left for New York City in a fourteen-foot U-Haul.

We didn't have a place to live. We did have our friend Karyn's uncle's phone number in case anything bad happened, but when you are twenty-two and headed out on an adventure, you believe you are invincible and things like an apartment or having someone to lean on seem irrelevant.

I couldn't get the truck out of the parking lot, so Casey ended up driving the entire way. There was a blindingly ferocious rainstorm in West Virginia; I accidentally lost Casey's contacts at a gas station stop in Pennsylvania; but after some white-knuckle driving into Manhattan, we made it. Without GPS. Now, keep in mind that I came to the city once at the age of sixteen on a church trip, and Casey had never been. Again: youth + naiveté = JUMP!

That night, we locked and parked the truck at the U-Haul rental on Twenty-third Street and made our way to Times Square to live in a hostel for the next couple of weeks (double-bunk beds shared with a couple from the Netherlands, and a mattress on the floor for the early-rising Brit). Everything was loud and bright and exciting and a blur. That's what happens when you take a leap: the ground rushes up to meet you and your instinct is to just brace for the impact and figure out everything else later. Sometimes it works, and sometimes it doesn't. It's not the target, it's the jump out of the plane door that matters.

But taking the leap doesn't have to be on the scale of a cross-country move. It can be anything: A new hairstyle. Considering starting the job search. Asking for what you are worth. Trying the weird thing on the menu. Deciding to have a child on your own. Choosing to slip your hand into your date's. That moment when you stop doing what you don't want to do. Finding a new hobby. Standing up for what you believe is right. Taking the leap to get it done.

There's a quote that is attributed (mistakenly) to Eleanor Roosevelt: "Do one thing every day that scares you." It's not a bad way to live, and recently my friend Sally said something akin to it that has stuck with me: "What got you here won't get you *there*." It's true. The moment is now, and tomorrow the moment will be different (never truer than in these difficult times). Perfect emotional bookends.

Bravery doesn't have a limit. Being scared is a fact of life. Big or small choices are waiting to be made. Take that step forward. What are you waiting for?

Happy-making things in a difficult world:

The power of dissent. The fact that light bulbs power an Easy-Bake Oven. That black-and-white 1993 Jose R. Lopez photo *Justice Ruth Bader Ginsburg on Her First Day on the Supreme Court.* That moment when your life cracks wide open. Not stepping on a sidewalk crack. Cracking open a bottle of Sancerre. Cleo Laine's recording of "I'm Beginning to See the Light." Chicken pot pie. The Fisher-Price Chatter Telephone. Warm croissants with jam and a cup of hot coffee. That January 23, 2013, *Smithsonian* magazine article by Karen Abbott, "Everything Was Fake but Her Wealth." Thinking a combine is moving quickly through a wheat field when it's actually going only about four miles per hour. Sifting the flour. "I can name that song in five notes." The fact that approximately thirty thousand quills cover a porcupine. Soft Cell's recording of "Tainted Love"—the extended version with "Where Did Our Love Go?" included at the end. The sizzling sound of something hitting a hot griddle. The haphazard way a small child sets the table. **The utterly bizarre and wonderful collection at the Mütter Museum** at the College of Physicians of Philadelphia. Entenmann's. A shaky connection that becomes a strong connection, figuratively or literally. A functioning player piano. The moment the watercolors blend. A broken-in Lands' End barn coat. That September 16, 2020, *Washington Post* Inspired Life article by Cathy Free, "She Was Homeless and Living in a Store's Parking Lot. Then the Store Hired Her." Roasted red peppers.

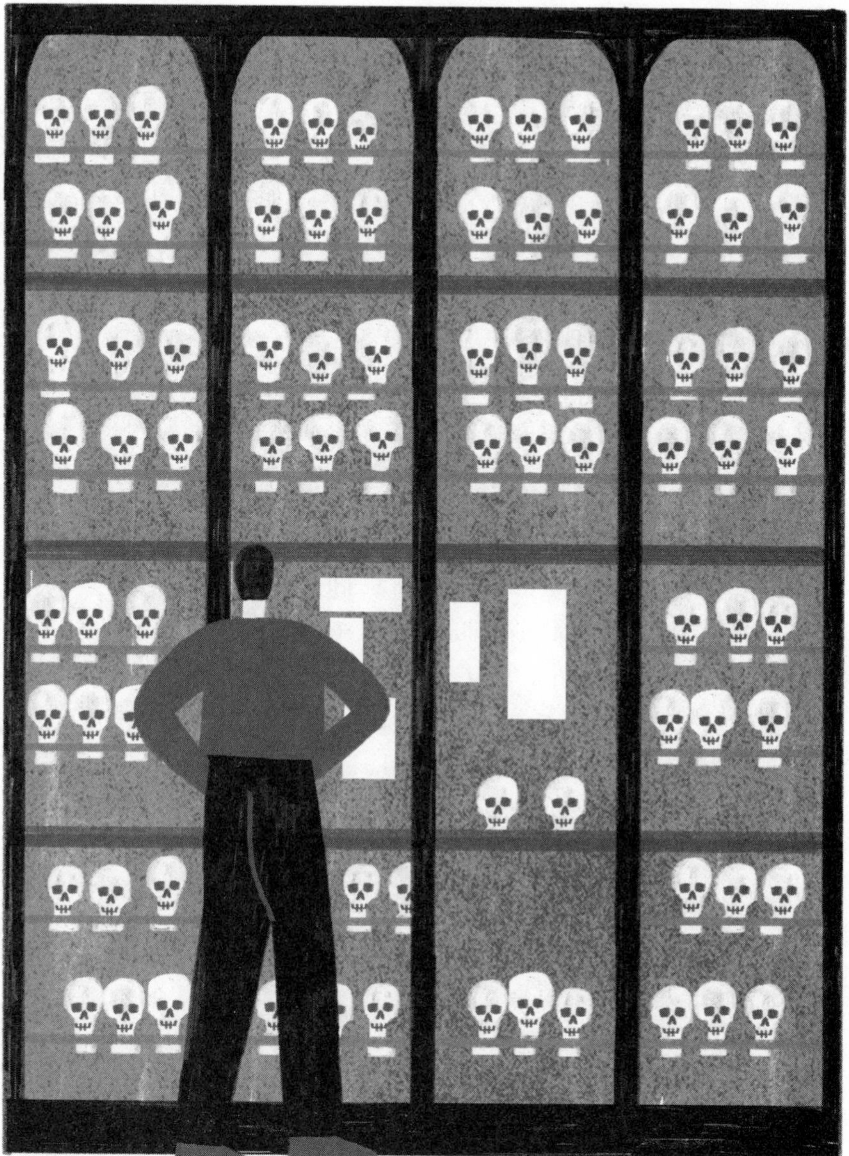

Happy-making things in a difficult world:
The rhythmic swish of a martini shaker. Ordering a dish in a restaurant that you would never make at home. Captain & Tennille's recording of "Love Will Keep Us Together." The fact that while **Saturn's ring** appears to be solid, there are actually multiple rings made up mostly of water-ice particles. Jia Tolentino's nonfiction *Trick Mirror: Reflections on Self-Delusion*. **Making the best of a bad situation.** That moment when you stop procrastinating and start doing. Ida O'Keeffe's 1933 painting *Tulips*. Laverne Cox, national treasure. John Glenn, national treasure. Gwen Ifill, national treasure. Astrud Gilberto's recording of "Summer Samba (So Nice)." The **strange fact** that Robert Todd Lincoln, son of the president, was saved in a near-fatal train platform accident by Edwin Booth, brother of the president's assassin, in late 1863 or early 1864. That 1950 Grandma Moses painting *The Quilting Bee*. Signature quilts. A filled autograph book. Manhattanhenge. The act of tumbling out of bed and stumbling to the kitchen and pouring yourself a cup of ambition and then yawning and stretching and trying to come to life. NPR's Tiny Desk Concerts. Haircut 100's recording of "Love Plus One." The 1986 New York Mets. **Swaddling the baby.** A sturdy laundry basket. The hiss of the iron. Bob Fosse's choreography for "Steam Heat."

The entire
score of
*In the
Heights.*

Happy-making things in a difficult world:

Pride. Popping a second piece of Wrigley's spearmint gum into your mouth along with the first. **Becoming friends with your mother-in-law.** That June 27, 2020, *New York Times* opinion piece by Laura Hillenbrand, "I Was in Love with a Tree That Swallowed the Sky." **Instant gratification.** Delayed gratification. The fact that in season 1 of *Sesame Street*, Oscar the Grouch was orange. Slimey. The Trash Can Sinatras' recording of "Obscurity Knocks." That 1939 Augusta Savage sculpture, *The Harp.* Richie and Joanie and Howard and Marion and Ralph Malph and Potsie and the Fonz. Garry Marshall, national treasure. Lionel Hampton, national treasure. Mildred Dresselhaus, national treasure. That July 1984 *Vanity Fair* article by George Plimpton, "Fireworks by Plimpton!" The fact that soil pH is the determining factor in hydrangea color. That Richard Avedon photo *Ronald Fischer, Beekeeper, Davis, California, May 9, 1981.* **A crash of rhinoceroses.** A knot of **toads.** A consortium of crabs. That January 31, 2020, episode of *This American Life*, "The Show of Delights." **An old tire swing. The monkey bars.** S. E. Hinton's novel *The Outsiders.* Having your choice of bunk beds. Margaret Whiting's recording of "A Fine Romance." Floppy hats on toddlers. A candle-lit birthday cake entering the room with a hush.

Happy-making things in a difficult world:

Sifting through the paint chips over and over and finally settling on a color. Benny Goodman's recording of "Sing, Sing, Sing." Looking at the stamps in your passport from the comfort of home. The Tiffany Yellow Diamond. Watch fobs. Prince's recording of "Little Red Corvette." Someone who says, "We need you." Someone who says, "You add value." That Rita Dove poem "Maple Valley Branch Library, 1967." Jack Buck, national treasure. Joseph Medicine Crow, national treasure. Gloria Estefan, national treasure. A long, laugh-filled phone call. Jane Hamilton's 1998 novel, *The Short History of a Prince*. Prince George. That *Everybody Loves Raymond* episode "Marie's Sculpture" (season 6, episode 5). Movie-themed slot machines. The candy aisle at the drugstore. Jack Otterson's 1939 *Vases* painting that adorned Frasier's apartment during the series' entire run. Martin's recliner. Paul and Jamie and Murray and Lisa and Ira and Fran and Mark. The entire *Pulp Fiction* soundtrack. The fact that the world's oldest breed of dog is the Saluki. The fact that the oldest dated violin is from 1564. The indoor street at the Winterthur Museum in Delaware. Frazier Chorus's recording of "Dream Kitchen." A quiver of cobras. A labor of moles. Ornate trivets. That 1994 Laura Aguilar photo *Bea and Myself.*

Happy-making things in a difficult world:
A Steinway baby grand Model S with its lid propped open. Hearing someone playing the piano through an open window as you walk by. That 1989 Herb Ritts photo *Djimon with Octopus, Hollywood.* **Making it home just before the skies open.** People who don't honk. Julie Andrews's recording of "I Have Confidence." Judy Woodruff's bookshelves on the PBS *NewsHour.* Valerie and Marky Mark and Mickey and Jane and Juna and Paulie G. and Tom and *I'm IT!* and *Room and Bored* and *The Comeback.* Audra McDonald's recording of "Stars and the Moon." The fact that the sun is actually a dwarf star. **Habitat for Humanity,** national treasure. Special Olympics, national treasure. The Trevor Project, national treasure. Those February 5, 2014, and May 4, 2020, *Fresh Air* interviews with Tim Gunn. *Hamilton* on Disney+. Sugar cookies with marbled icing. That 2017 Henry Taylor painting *Cicely and Miles Visit the Obamas.* **A flamboyance of flamingos.** A coalition of cheetahs. A shiver of sharks.

Happy-making things in a difficult world:

Dinner overlooking the ocean. All of those 2020 Emmy wins for *Schitt's Creek*. The last day of work before vacation. **Ordering the soufflé for dessert** at the same time that you order your appetizer and entrée. The Look Human pullover hoodie emblazoned with "I JUST MET YOU AND THIS IS CRAZY BUT HERE'S MY LABYRINTH I STOLE YOUR BABY." **Emptying the library cart.** The fact that the Mississippi River is more than eleven miles wide at its widest point. Madonna's recording of "Rain." Nelson Riddle, national treasure. Billy Porter, national treasure. Henrietta Lacks, national treasure. Maroon 5's recording of "Sugar." Acoustic versions of pop songs that reveal the actual strength of previously-thought-of-as-frivolous songs. Penelope and Elena and Lydia and Alex and Schneider. That 1953 Harry Callahan photo *Lake Michigan*. **That ever-present conundrum** "Why don't people with a British accent keep it when they sing?" Dunder Mifflin. Closets, Closets, Closets, Closets. Kramer's Kandy Kitchen. **A warm pan of Rice Krispies treats.** St. Jude Children's Research Hospital. Ronald McDonald House Charities. The Humane Society of the United States. That 1889 Louise Catherine Breslau painting *Lesende*. Quick visits. Long stays.

Happy-making things in a difficult world:
Sam Cooke's recording of "Summertime." Staining the deck. Roof decks.
That Bev Grant photo *Coney Island: July 4, 1968.* **Balancing the canoe as the second person settles.** Walley World.
Kellerman's. West Egg and East Egg. That 1960 Edward Hopper painting *Second Story Sunlight.* Red, white, and blue bunting. That 1925 Langston Hughes poem "Summer Nights." The art of Bernie Fuchs. The fact that **one pound of honey** requires a single bee to fly approximately ninety thousand miles to gather nectar. André Aciman's 2007 novel, *Call Me by Your Name.* Oliver's billowy blue shirt. That 1868 Renoir painting *In Summer.* **Sparklers twirling in the dark.** Mariah Carey's recording of "Vision of Love." A field of goldenrod. "The corn is as high as an elephant's eye." That moment when the mosquito bite stops itching. That moment when you step off the sweltering platform and into a freezing-cold subway car.
The Jersey Shore.

Things You Might Consider Doing Today

Plant a kaleidoscope butterfly bush. Watch the Netflix documentary *Crip Camp: A Disability Revolution.* Mail some old photos to the people who are in them. Look at that 2013 painting by Charlie Buckley *Old Sardis—Summer Storm.* **Go to Wendy's and get a Frosty. Pick up some Dunkin' Munchkins for breakfast.** Listen to Patti LuPone's recording of "Being Alive." Read that September 1994 *American Heritage* article by Carl Sferrazza Anthony, "Love, Jackie," which describes the friendship between Jacqueline Onassis and Lady Bird Johnson. Watch "Time Enough at Last," the season 1, episode 8 of *The Twilight Zone.* Think of a dish you love to eat but have never cooked before, and then go make it for dinner. Read that May 16, 2018, *Vogue* article by Katie Berrington, "Jesmyn Ward on Weathering Rejection and Finding Her Stories." **Sit in a hammock. Sit on a park bench.** Blast Rihanna's "We Found Love" and start dancing. Google image search "Joshua Tree + sunset." Look at that 2015 photo by Luis Alberto Rodriguez *Josh and Jermaine.* Buy a small aquarium and some fantail guppies. Buy two books on subjects you've never read about. Buy someone a pick-me-up gift. Look on YouTube for "Joe Namath Super Bowl III Highlights." Celebrate the day. Celebrate making it through the week. Celebrate all of the good in the world, even when it seems hard to do so. And then rinse and repeat after me:

"Your future is whatever you make it. So make it a good one."

Road Trips

We road-tripped everywhere during my childhood and throughout college in various vehicles: Dad's van for summer trips to the beaches of Florida and South Carolina. Jason Bradley's parents' car for a high school spring break drive across the plains to the still-snowy mountains of Colorado. A fall drive in my old Ford Escort down to Metropolis, Illinois, back when the gambling riverboat left the dock and took a short trip down the Mississippi River.

Road trips are full of promise. Your destination far out of reach, yet waiting, and the mileage accounted for.

You've packed the snacks, possibly junk food you wouldn't normally eat: Hostess CupCakes. Trail mix. Pringles. You've packed the drinks, each person requesting their favorite: Coke. AriZona Iced Tea. Gatorade.

Games in the car at the ready for the long stretch of road ahead: Uno. Slug Bug. Candy Land. Blankets and pillows piled high, arranged in every corner, books, and a flashlight prepped for nighttime reading. Directions and driving slots and chosen seats planned. Mixtapes and playlists curated, or, back in the day, finding a new radio station as the current one begins to crackle, songs static filled and lyrics jumbled as you hurtle forward.

Long stretches of silence as strangely named streets and roads not taken whiz by. Intimate conversations that happen while others are fast asleep. The drive-throughs. The pit stops. The rest stops providing a stretch, next to people you may or may not pass later on the road.

And then the final countdown as you reach the target: vacation, or a family visit, or the trip back home. The cozy, often long leg of the journey is over, and the next part of the trip is about to begin.

What has been a memorable road trip for you? What did you read? What did you eat? And what was the one song you played on repeat and sang loudest to?

The fact that the melting of the Wicked Witch of the West is never explained yet quickly accepted.

Happy-making things in a difficult world:

A dusting of snow on the front gate. A lit-up china cabinet in a dark dining room. Mallomars. Rickie Lee Jones's recording of "Lush Life." **A restaurant's private room used for a family celebration.** The Grand Salon at Newport's Marble House. Amanda Mackenzie Stuart's 2005 nonfiction, *Consuelo and Alva Vanderbilt: The Story of a Daughter and a Mother in the Gilded Age.* Marilyn Milian, national treasure. Hal Prince, national treasure. Shirley Chisholm, national treasure. That September 20, 2020, *Washington Post* KidsPost article by Jason Bittel, "Ever Wondered Why Trees Ditch Their Leaves Each Fall?" **Bannerman Castle.** The **Magic Castle. King Friday's Castle.** Tuttorosso tomato paste. Putting up the decorations far in advance of the actual holiday. Nandor and Laszlo and Nadja and Guillermo and Colin Robinson. **Old, worn mallard decoys.** Appropriately positioned wall sconces. That 1994 Joan Marcus photo *Cast of Rent.* Fork and napkin on the left; knife, spoon, and glass on the right. A house or building with a porte-cochere. Jordan Allen-Dutton, Jason Catalano, Gregory J. Qaiyum, Jeffrey Qaiyum, and Erik Wiener's play, *The Bomb-Itty of Errors.* **Autocorrect, except when it doesn't get the word right.** The ding of the typewriter bell when the margin is met. The churn of the mimeograph. The San Francisco 49ers. 425 Lafayette Street, NYC. 818 South Second Street, Minneapolis. 2910 La Jolla Village Drive, La Jolla.

Happy-making things in a difficult world:

Date night at home. Dressing up for a date night out. Scoring a reservation you didn't think you'd get. Violent Femmes' recording of "Blister in the Sun." That June 29, 2020, *New York Times* article by Benjamin Lowy, "Swimming with the Sea Lions of Los Islotes." Google image search "Machu Picchu + Sun Gate sunrise." **That moment when the fireworks stop. That moment when the overture starts.** Rhiannon Giddens's recording of "She's Got You." Expertly navigating the riding lawn mower. All-star games. That 1978 Olga Abizu painting *900-50-80*. Marian Anderson, national treasure. Mary Lasker, national treasure. Bill Russell, national treasure. Someone who says, "Wanna hear some gossip?" Someone who says, "Let bygones be bygones." Someone who says, "Once upon a time . . ." Louise and George and Lionel and Helen and Tom and Jenny and Florence and Mother Jefferson and Bentley. That 1993 Chuck Baird painting *Art No. 2*. The pizza joint that recognizes your voice when you call to place an order. Warm blueberry pie with vanilla ice cream. The fact that Route 66 is 2,448 miles long and runs through only eight states. Scrunchies. Spandau Ballet's recording of "True."

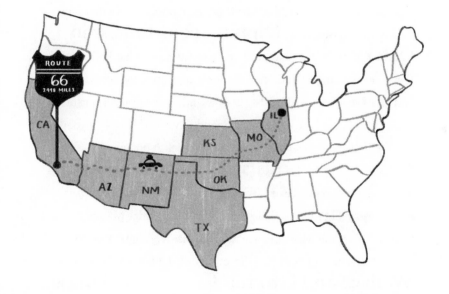

Happy-making things in a difficult world:

A long hike that you've done countless times before. That *Mame* quote "Life is a banquet, and most poor suckers are starving to death!" That amazing story that Matthew Rosenberg posted on Twitter after Carl Reiner passed away. **Dipping your fingers in water** to shape the final touch on the sandcastle. That 1947 Jacob Lawrence painting *The Builders*. Caramel apples. Candy corn. **Charlie Brown's shirt.** Cyndi Lauper's recording of "You Don't Know." Jack and Rebecca and Kevin and Kate and Toby and Randall and Beth and William and Miguel. A bouquet of astilbe. A good prognosis. The fact that the 1831 London Bridge now stands in Lake Havasu City, Arizona. That July 16, 2019, *Paris Review* essay "The Crane Wife," by CJ Hauser. Marlee Matlin, national treasure. Margaret McNamara, national treasure. August Wilson, national treasure. Shirley Horn's recording of "I Thought About You." **Wallace and Gromit. Kermit and Fozzie.** Ashburn and Mullins. That 1986 Lorna Simpson photo *Waterbearer*. Your high school freshman year photo. Sleeping in study hall. Jacquelyn Mitchard's 1996 novel, *The Deep End of the Ocean*. The entire score of *Jurassic Park*. The original cast of *A Chorus Line*. The symmetry of scaffolding.

Happy-making things in a difficult world:

Summer temperatures in Scotland. Episode 13 of *Conductor Cam* by Rob McClure. Chuck Wendig's Twitter. Anything that makes you question your beliefs and then reaffirms or changes them. All of those many, many **reasons to get out of bed in the morning.** An empty, yet stained, inkwell. Elton John's recording of "I Guess That's Why They Call It the Blues." George Rodrigue's 1990s series of *Blue Dog* paintings. **A six-on-two double-breasted suit jacket.** Lorelai and Rory and Luke and Emily and Richard and Sookie and Lane and Michel. That 1937 Gluck painting *Medallion*. Serena Williams's four aces in a row at Wimbledon 2012. That Groucho Marx quote "Time flies like an arrow; fruit flies like a banana." Interest earned on a savings account. A balanced checkbook. Fortune Feimster's Netflix comedy special, *Sweet and Salty*. Library books on hold just for you. **The Noguchi Museum, Queens.** Louise Nevelson's 1982 sculpture *Sky Cathedral*. Someone who says, **"I'm listening."** Someone who says, "I hear you." Someone who says, **"Start from the top and tell me again."** Pharrell's recording of and video for "Happy." Katharine Hepburn and Spencer Tracy. Ossie Davis and Ruby Dee. Matt Bomer and Simon Halls. Sarah Paulson and Holland Taylor. The Backstreet Boys' recording of "I Want It That Way." Seizing the moment. "Finishing the hat."

MIXTAPE:
Rainy Saturday

There's nothing better than staying inside on a rainy, gloomy day. Naps, games, getting cozy, something cooking in the Crock-Pot, and watching an old movie that you love are some must-dos for a day that requires hunkering down. Here is a mixtape to help settle you into an indoors mood.

A	B
"Blue Savannah" –Erasure	"Landslide" –The Chicks
"The Man That Got Away" (live at Carnegie Hall) –Judy Garland	"Sooner or Later" (live) –Bernadette Peters
"The Killing Moon" –Echo and the Bunnymen	"I've Heard That Song Before" –Harry James
"Mad World" –Seal	"Let the River Run" –The St. Thomas Choir of Men and Boys
"Summertime" –Sam Cooke	
"Better Than Anything" –Irene Kral with the Junior Mance Trio	"Autumn in New York" –Billie Holiday
	"America the Beautiful" –Ray Charles
"I Happen to Like New York" –Bobby Short	"Galileo" –Indigo Girls
"Halley Came to Jackson" –Mary Chapin Carpenter	"Harvest Moon" –Cassandra Wilson
	"What a Little Moonlight Can Do" (live) –Diana Ross
"A Little Time" –The Beautiful South	
"Si tu vois ma mère (Slow)" –Sidney Bechet	"Moonlight in Vermont" –Stan Getz and Astrud Gilberto

The Green Room at the White House.

Happy-making things in a difficult world:

That October 6, 2008, *Vanity Fair* archive "Dominick Dunne's Quarter-Century." A Lemon Drop Martini. The Lemonheads' recording of "Mrs. Robinson." Ina Garten's recipe for lemon curd. **Paying in cash. The day the layaway is paid off.** The day the credit card is paid off. Signaling a wordless "We'll take the check." That dress made up of 254 Gold AmEx cards worn by Lizzy Gardiner at the 1995 Oscars, where she won for Best Costume Design. Camila Cabello and Daddy Yankee's recording of "Havana." David Gonzalez's July 10, 2020, *New York Times* article celebrating the work of MTA photographer Patrick Cashin, "Think You've Seen the Subway? Not Like This You Haven't." **The last day of jury duty.** A fresh dish towel. An extra-sudsy bath. A breeze through a metal screen door. Classic gas pumps. Referees making the right call. A fully returned security deposit. Addresses that contain a PO box. That 1925 Gerald Murphy painting *Watch*. Andy Samberg's dimples. Sterling K. Brown's smile. Phyllis Diller's laugh. Changing the batteries in the smoke detectors. Friends who have a pool. A follow spot. A second encore. John Leguizamo's play *Freak*. Someone who says, **"Listen to your instincts."** Someone who says, **"Call me if you need me."** Someone who says, "No one will notice."

The Gherkin in London.

The Sail Hotel in Barcelona.

The Grande Arche in Paris.

That June 28, 1956, *New York Times* photo by Meyer Liebowitz, *Francine Monath of Bergenfield, N.J., Giving Final Instructions to Her 5-Year-Old-Son, Steven, at Grand Central Terminal.*

A night at the rodeo.

A day at the amusement park.

The Bee Girl in Blind Melon's video for "No Rain."

Happy-making things in a difficult world:
A wall-mounted rotary phone with an extra-long cord. A trustworthy babysitter. The day you make an offer on the house. **The day the mortgage is paid off.** Copper pipes. Slate roofs. Your favorite art house movie theater. Community theater. That 1990 Herbert Singleton carved painting *Love That Not Love*. Someone who says, "Today's specials are . . ." Someone who says, "You are special." The *Abbott and Costello Meet* . . . various horror monsters series of films. Jerry and Elaine and George and Kramer. **The Strokes' recording of "The Adults Are Talking."** A feeling of accomplishment. A feeling of belonging. Nancy Milford's 2001 nonfiction, *Savage Beauty: The Life of Edna St. Vincent Millay*. K-Swiss Classic VN tennis shoes. Jason Reitman's fan-film version of *The Princess Bride*. A progressive dinner that ends at your house for dessert. The entire score of *Fun Home*. A nuisance of cats. An army of herring. A thunder of hippopotamuses. The cacophony of playing Hungry Hungry Hippos. Watching the parade of hats at the Kentucky Derby.

Happy-making things in a difficult world:

A day at the beach spent under an umbrella with a packed cooler nearby. The Sunday Routine column in *The New York Times*. Turning on the first lamp of the evening. Turning out all the lights and heading to bed. *Masterpiece Theatre*. Meramec Caverns, Stanton, Missouri. Mammoth Cave, Edmonson County, Kentucky. General Public's recording of "Tenderness." Quickly finding the lost item you desperately need. The story of how that 1954 Norman Rockwell painting *Breaking Home Ties* was bought in 1960 by Don Trachte Jr. for $900, hidden behind a fake wall for forty-five years, and then sold by his heirs for $15.4 million in 2006. The fact that the Great Barrier Reef consists of three thousand separate reefs and nine hundred islands of coral. R.E.M.'s recording of "Nightswimming." That 1954–1955 Jasper Johns painting *Flag*. Ruby Bridges, national treasure. Ryan White, national treasure. Edward Albee, national treasure. Lizzo's recording of "Truth Hurts." A sneeze that doesn't happen. Accurate weather forecasts. A smack of jellyfish. A cete of badgers. A wake of buzzards. That January 2011 "Honey Badger" YouTube video. Hitchcock's use of the MacGuffin.

Things You Might Consider Saying to Someone Today

Just a note to tell you how wonderful you are. **Thank you** for taking a chance on me all those years ago when I applied for the job. **Thank you** for getting me through some very hard times. **Thank you** for throwing me that party. **Thank you** for teaching me to never give up on someone you believe in. **Thank you** for showing me how to be an amazing partner. **Thank you** for your incredible laugh. **Thank you** for showing me the value of wanderlust and travel. **Thank you** for showing me the importance of family. **Thank you** for showing me how to make the tough call with grace. **Thank you** for showing me how to keep going. **Thank you** for teaching me that saying no is okay. **Thank you** for your example of how to be a wonderful friend. You are a magical creature and we are all so lucky to have you in our lives.

Someone who says,

"I saw it and knew you had to have it."

Happy-making things in a difficult world:

A silver anniversary. A sapphire anniversary. A platinum anniversary. The gilt-edged Scully & Scully *Merriam-Webster Thesaurus*. Scrooge McDuck. *Scrooged*. Skipping school for a day. Perfect attendance. Hitting it out of the park, literally or figuratively. Karl Jenkins's recording of "Cantus Inaqualis." Adopting an older mutt. A yardstick with a lumber-supply logo affixed to the front. Banned Books Week. That Cleo Wade poem "Does the Sea Ever Say." Perfectly aligned orange construction cones stretching into the horizon. **Mood boards. Mood rings.** A bad mood that becomes a good mood. That Neal Boenzi photo *New York, 1966*. Potted herbs growing on the kitchen window ledge. The chef's exactly measured mise en place in a cooking show. Enigma's recording of "Push the Limits." Jim Henson's *The Storyteller*. Imagining that the trash can is a basketball hoop. **Dog-earing the pages.** Removing the dust jacket as you read the hardcover. Inclusivity. The Diane von Furstenberg wrap dress. The 1954 Mercedes SL 300 Gullwing. A garden apartment. The fact that a caterpillar's body is made up of more than four thousand muscles. Jerry Rice's 208 touchdowns. That 1650 painting by Jan Asselijn, *The Threatened Swan*. Stefon. Rolling up your sleeves. Opening the can of Pillsbury biscuits with a thwack against the counter edge. Mastering the game face.

Happy-making things in a difficult world:

Gratitude. *Clueless*. The eternal youth of Paul Rudd. Hummingbirds buzzing about. Going out on Friday night. Staying in on Saturday night. **The Oculus. The Dakota. The Ansonia.** The first (and each subsequent) bite of Martha Stewart's pasta with spinach pesto and ricotta recipe. Chita Rivera, national treasure. The Rock, national treasure. Caroline Kennedy, national treasure. **Blanket forts.** Peggy Parish's Amelia Bedelia novels. Jif smooth peanut butter slathered on a freshly toasted English muffin. Lillias White's bring-down-the-house solo in "Brotherhood of Man" from *How to Succeed in Business Without Really Trying*. The idea of living in a tiny cabin in the middle of the woods in the middle of an island in the middle of a lake. The art of Garth Williams. The art of Pauline Baynes. The art of procrastination. Cracking the window so that your bedroom is just the tiniest bit chilly. **Reading in bed. Reading in bed in the middle of the night.** That Cadbury Egg "Easter Bunny Tryouts" commercial. High school letter jackets. Watching *The Godfather* and *The Godfather Part II* and pretending the movies end there. A savory dessert. That March 2, 2015, J. R. Moehringer *ESPN* magazine cover story, "The Education of Alex Rodriguez." **Dogs with bandanas around their necks.** The Morgan Library. Peter, Susan, Edmund, and Lucy. And Mr. Tumnus. Pressing a leaf between two heavy books. Cleaning as you go when you cook. Long-gone department stores such as Bendel, Gimbels, Marshall Field's, and B. Altman. Ella Fitzgerald and Louis Armstrong's recording of "Moonlight in Vermont." Family get-togethers where everyone hangs out in the kitchen. Diner placemats consisting of local ads. The meditative act of separating the egg yolks and whites.

Happy-making things in a difficult world:
Billy Wilder, national treasure. Gloria Steinem, national treasure.
Madeline Swegle, national treasure. **"Go forth and kick butt."** The Netflix documentary *Mucho Mucho Amor: The Legend of Walter Mercado.* **Knowing your worth.** Seeing someone else's value and showing it to them when they cannot see it for themselves. Carrie Underwood's recording of "Thank God for Hometowns." Water towers festooned with the city name. A morning with the newspaper, a pot of coffee, and a piece of crisp toast with a slather of butter and Smucker's strawberry jelly. Seal's recording of "Mad World." **Having just enough gift wrap and Scotch tape to finish the presents.** That 1991 Lenore Chinn painting *The Family.* The main stained-glass window at the Phillips Church, which was built in 1895 at Exeter. Jude and Willem and Malcolm and JB. The day that you realize the potty training is complete. That Johanne Rahaman photo *Downtown West Palm Beach, Florida, 2015.* The law office of Annalise Keating. The law firm of McKenzie, Brackman, Chaney and Kuzak. The law firm of Reddick, Boseman & Lockhart. **Taking a flight of stairs two steps at a time.**

Happy-making things in a difficult world:
That Orson Welles quote "If you want a happy ending, that depends, of course, on where you stop your story." Klondike bars. A dollop of Daisy. That 2017 Carmen Herrera painting *Equilibrio*. That story of how college student Carolyn Davidson quickly designed the Nike swoosh in 1971. **A summer tan. Sun-kissed cheeks.** That February 1996 *Vanity Fair* cover article on Emma Thompson, "Never Look Back." The sitcom laugh track. Mike and Carol and Greg and Peter and Bobby and Marcia and Jan and Cindy and Alice. Rob Base and DJ E-Z Rock's recording of "It Takes Two." A perfectly executed backflip. Climbing the ladder up to the high dive. Adam Gopnik's 2000 nonfiction, *Paris to the Moon.* **A game of Hacky Sack. A game of badminton.** Wiping down the kitchen counters after the dishes are done. Rena Silverman's October 12, 2017, *New York Times* article, "The Subway Portraits of Helen Levitt." Perfectly packing the trunk the night before an early-morning road trip. House of Pain's recording of "Jump Around."

Happy-making things in a difficult world:

The crunchy sound a lawn mower makes when mowing over small sticks. Belleek Basketweave china. Red Solo cups. That September 3, 2020, *New York Times* article by Rachel Nuwer, "A Turtle with a Permanent Smile Was Brought Back from Near Extinction." **Chewing on the cap of a BIC Cristal ballpoint pen during class.** An amber L. E. Smith glass turkey. Sharing the spotlight. The yearly "Blessing of the Animals" at the Cathedral of St. John the Divine. That September 23, 2020, *Washington Post* Inspired Life column by Sydney Page, "A Farmer Fell Ill. So Dozens of His Neighbors Showed Up Spontaneously and Harvested His Crops." **Unexpected victories. Unexpected visitors.** Rocking the baby to sleep and then sitting together a little while longer. The 13,171 miles that make up the length of the Great Wall of China. The 605 feet that make up the height of the Space Needle. The eleven inches that make up the length of a football. **A good massage.** Someone who scratches your back. Liberace's candelabra. Renata Tebaldi's recording of "O mio babbino caro." Winding the clock. **Casting a fly rod.** President Bartlet and Leo and Josh and Toby and Sam and C.J. and Charlie and Donna and Abbey. The entire score of *Kiss Me, Kate.* Carefully opening the cardboard tab on a new box of Kleenex. Shonda Rhimes, national treasure. Mikhail Baryshnikov, national treasure. That 1924 George Bellows painting *Dempsey and Firpo.* **Using the bellows to stoke the fire.**

That Song . . .
You Know the One

Summer 1995. One of my then roommates brings home a new album. Begins to play it relentlessly. It is angry. It is loud. It is someone screeching. The lyrics are weird. And I hate it. But months later I find myself limping through a bad breakup, and somehow Alanis Morissette's album *Jagged Little Pill*, which ended up in my CD collection when I moved, is no longer a nuisance but a lifeline (as it was for millions of others).

Do you ever have those days when you can't remember what you did twenty-four hours before, but if you are listening to an album or song you love, the lyrics—and feelings and memories the songs represent—come back without a second thought? Even decades later? We all have them, shaped by experience, movies and television shows, recommendations, or, best of all, by accidental discovery.

The beauty of a piece of art—a song you know every word to all these years later, that photo you keep close by, this painting that still calls to you, the film you've watched a thousand times yet turn to again and again—is that it becomes a shared object between you and the creator.

Music, however, packs an especially emotional wallop—it's like a sensory memory that can take you back to that instant in its entirety. The spot you were in when you first heard it. The person you were with. The way you listened—streaming, 8-track, CDs, Walkman, vinyl.

The breakup you didn't think you'd survive. The first love. Your high school senior prom. The day the baby comes home. A fiftieth anniversary. Your best friend's wedding. That first holiday without someone you love. Your grandma's favorite song. Your sibling's terrible taste in music. That epic college party.

What is the song that takes you back to an important moment in your life? What is the song that means the most to you?

The *Vanity Fair*
Proust Questionnaire
column.

◇

Oprah's *O Magazine*
What I Know for Sure
column.

◇

The fact that
Ann Landers and
Dear Abby
were twin sisters.

Happy-making things in a difficult world:
Paul and Julia. Gabrielle and Ashley. Ina and Jeffrey. Ina Garten's roasted eggplant Parmesan recipe. That 2018 Zanele Muholi photo *Ngwane I, Oslo*. The sizzle of grilled peaches. Outdoor patio lanterns. **Small-Business Saturday. Independent Bookstore Day.** Annie Lennox's recording of "A Thousand Beautiful Things." Smaug. **Drogon. Norbert.** Someone who says, "What do you need?" Someone who says, "Let me help." Stacy Schiff's 2010 nonfiction, *Cleopatra: A Life*. The satisfying first crunch of a ruby-red McIntosh apple. **That rare yellow turtle** discovered in India on October 27, 2020. Donna Lewis's recording of "I Love You Always Forever." That 2010 Frank Romero painting *Harbor Freeway*. The determination of a first-year grad student. The long view of a nonagenarian. **A congregation of alligators. A bed of clams.** A pod of dolphins. The fact that Hedy Lamarr was also an inventor and patent owner of spread-spectrum radio. The entire score of *She Loves Me*.

Things You Might Need to Hear Today

"Here comes the sun" (the Beatles). "No day but today" (*Rent*). "Carpe diem" (*Dead Poets Society*). "Nolite te bastardes carborundorum" (*The Handmaid's Tale*). **"There's no place like home"** (*The Wizard of Oz*). "Smiling's my favorite" (*Elf*). "A Jedi uses the Force for knowledge and defense, never for attack" (*The Empire Strikes Back*). "Katherine Johnson knew: once you took the first step, anything was possible" (*Hidden Figures*). **"Everything's impossible until somebody does it"** (*Batman*). "Screws fall out all the time. The world's an imperfect place" (*The Breakfast Club*). "Sometimes you have to look hard at a person and realize he's doing the best he can" (*On Golden Pond*). "Go the distance" (*Field of Dreams*). "I got through all of last year" (*Follies*). "No one is alone" (*Into the Woods*). "Yes, everything was beautiful at the ballet" (*A Chorus Line*). "Don't let's ask for the moon. We have the stars" (*Now, Voyager*). "You'll have bad times, but it'll always wake you up to the good stuff you weren't paying attention to" (*Good Will Hunting*). "Goodnight you princes of Maine, you kings of New England" (*The Cider House Rules*). And the best advice I ever received, from my amazing grandma Peggy when I was whining about something or other during my visit on the day after Christmas 2013: "You're gonna have to be like your grandma.

You're gonna have to Get. Tough."

Happy-making things in a difficult world:
That 2015 Theron Humphrey photo *1974 BMW R90*. The French
Quarter. **Anne Rice's former New Orleans
house at 1239 First Street and Prytania,**
which was also the home of the Mayfair family in *The Witching Hour*.
Someone who makes you a cocktail.
Someone who makes you feel seen. The Cure's
recording of "Pictures of You." Pencils with sayings printed on them.
"Don't you love New York in the fall? It makes me wanna buy school
supplies. I would send you a bouquet of newly sharpened pencils if I
knew your name and address. On the other hand, this not knowing has
its charms." That Marcel Antonisse photo *Miles Davis and Cicely Tyson
in the Netherlands, 1982.* A one-traffic-light town. A
coatrack overwhelmed with your guests' coats. **The smell of a
woodburning stove.** Jon Secada's recording of "Just
Another Day." Charles Bridge. Millennium Bridge. Glenfinnan
Viaduct. *The New Yorker* cartoons. That 2014 Steven Young Lee
porcelain *Vase with Landscape and Dinosaurs.* **Rescuing a
ladybug** in the house and setting it free outside. That August 14,
2015, *New York Times Magazine* essay "Oliver Sacks: Sabbath."

Happy-making things in a difficult world:

That moment when you decide to save the champagne cork as a tangible reminder of the reason for the celebration. That **Martina Navratilova** quote "Just go out there and do what you have to do." Sylvia Mendez, national treasure. S. E. Hinton, national treasure. David Rakoff, national treasure. Nena's recording of "99 Luftballons." Multiple snow days. The moment after the snow plow is gone. The "Three Utilities Problem." The "Three Cups Problem." The "Seven Bridges of Königsberg" problem. That John Bramblitt painting *Two Dogs*. **An intense game of Ping-Pong. A marathon game of Monopoly.** That moment when you clear your eyes and focus for the first time in the morning. Nicki Minaj's recording of "Super Bass." The excitement of the newly engaged. **The perspective of a long-married couple.** The act of opening a can of Pringles. Sticking a Bugle onto each of your five fingers. Sarah McLachlan's acoustic recording of "Possession." A. S. Byatt's 1990 novel, *Possession*. The fact that Christopher Plummer was the oldest actor to win an Oscar (at age eighty-two) and *then* Anthony Hopkins beat that record (at age eighty-three). The fact that Charlotte Cooper Sterry was the oldest female Wimbledon singles champion (at age thirty-seven). That 2018 Bisa Butler quilt painting *The Mighty Gents*. **A horseshoe hanging over the door for good luck.** The Cartier "LOVE" bracelet. That November 12, 2013, *Fresh Air* interview with Allie Brosh. Accurately naming the "New 7 Wonders of the World." The entire score of *A Strange Loop*. Froot Loops.

Happy-making things in a difficult world:
The fact that Central Park covers 843 acres filled with more than 19,000 trees and 9,000 benches. The fact that Bette Midler's New York Restoration project has saved more than 400 acres of **New York City's parks.** Taylor Swift and Bon Iver's recording of "Exile" (and the entire *Folklore* album). That story behind the two skulls resting in Haydn's tomb. **Shared birthdays. Shared milkshakes. A firm, but not too firm, handshake.** Old-fashioned barbershop chairs. That 1995 Len Prince photo *Matt LeBlanc, Hollywood.* The moment after the cold front pushes through. The fact that a nickel weighs more than a hummingbird. French onion dip. Fondue. Beverly Cleary's 1983 novel, *Dear Mr. Henshaw.* **When the game goes into overtime.** Lisa Loeb and Nine Stories' recording of "Do You Sleep?" Willie Mays, national treasure. Gwen Verdon, national treasure. Suzan Shown Harjo, national treasure. Ariel Levy's June 29, 2009, *New Yorker* profile of Nora Ephron, "Nora Knows What to Do." That 1931 Grant Wood painting *The Midnight Ride of Paul Revere.* **Addressing the last of the invitations.** Using up every last scrap of fabric. One for the road. Someone who says, "I've been right where you are." Someone who says, **"That's fixable."** Someone who says, "Hang up your hat." The entire score of *Little Shop of Horrors.*

Happy-making things in a difficult world:

Michael Schulman's July 26, 2020, *New Yorker* interview, "'Theatre Can't Miss This Moment': An Interview with Audra McDonald." **A red Radio Flyer wagon. The Fisher-Price Bubble Mower.** Cleaning out the fireplace ashes the morning after a long night in front of the fire. Peter Gabriel's recording of "In Your Eyes." The Women's Rights Pioneers Monument, featuring Sojourner Truth, Susan B. Anthony, and Elizabeth Cady Stanton—sculpted by Meredith Bergmann. The 1,771 pieces that make up the LEGO Yoda. Florence + the Machine's recording of "Dog Days Are Over." The moment after you exit the corn maze. The moment after your presentation ends. *Spy.* The fact that Olympus Mons, on the planet Mars, is the biggest volcano in the solar system, measuring 16 miles high and 374 miles across. *Can You Ever Forgive Me?* **Family cheering you on from the sidelines.** Fanny packs. Finding the secret door to a speakeasy. Your [insert favorite sports team] jersey. The quiet of a late-night drive. Prince's recording of "Raspberry Beret." Unwrapping a Hershey bar with no breakage. Someone who says, "You did good." Someone who says, "Push yourself harder." TuTchT's 2016 painting *Tony's History.*

Happy-making things **in a difficult world:**

That 1971 Ron Galella photo *Jacqueline Kennedy Onassis and Aristotle Onassis at P. J. Clarke's Restaurant, New York, 1971.* **Commemorative plates. County fairs.** Craig Brown's 2018 nonfiction, *Ninety-Nine Glimpses of Princess Margaret.* That moment when the chairs are pulled out almost simultaneously and everyone sits down to dinner together. Hans Zimmer's recording of "Spider Pig." Arranging photos in photo albums. **A grilled cheese and tomato soup lunch** with a good magazine. That August 8, 2019, *New Yorker* Postscript by Hilton Als, "Toni Morrison's Truth." **Double-height windows.** Ivy climbing the brick facade. The fact that a cricket's ears are found on its legs. Calle 13's recording of and video for "Así de Grandes Son las Ideas." Any occasion that calls for a multitiered cake. Robin's-egg blue. Virginia Woolf's Monk's House. That 2015 Lillian Blades painting *Abundancescape.* **That moment the bride starts walking down the aisle.** Someone who says, "Find your happiness." The smell of sawdust in a woodshop. Stevie Wonder's recording of "We Can Work It Out."

Things You Might Consider Doing Today

Part your hair on the opposite side. Read that Julia de Burgos poem "Poem Detained in a Daybreak." Listen to the most recent episode of *The Best of Car Talk* podcast. Buy some handkerchiefs and start carrying one in your pocket. Watch that Hallmark movie *A Valentine's Match*. Watch Kurosawa's *Ran*. **Test-drive a car** even if you have no intention of buying one. Read that February 10, 2014, Onward and Outward *New Yorker* column by Roger Angell, "This Old Man: Life in the Nineties." **Clean out your coffee maker with vinegar.** Look up the April 14, 1912, evening menu on the *Titanic*. Make Hunt's Manwich Sloppy Joe Cornbread Bake recipe for supper. Buy a computer skin of your favorite photo for your laptop. Listen to the Indigo Girls' recording of "Galileo." **Scrub down the shower.** Start reading Elizabeth Marshall Thomas's 1993 nonfiction, *The Hidden Life of Dogs*. Restring the Weed Eater. Think about your favorite kind of day and then make it happen. **Google image search "sunset + Easter Island."** Don't do the laundry. Listen to Roy Eldridge's recording of "Rockin' Chair." **Relive a special moment in your life** and say "Thank you" after. Regroup. Recharge. Then take a deep breath. And then rinse and repeat after me:

"Go get 'em, tiger."

Happy-making things in a difficult world:

A fully replied-to email in-box. A box of Russell Stover candies. Not opening the Pandora's box. A-frame houses. Maira Kalman's illustrated version of Strunk and White's *The Elements of Style*. Therapy animals. A good therapist with a comfy couch. Someone who waits to pick you up at the station even when the train is very late. Closing the place down. Switching the sign to OPEN. Old metal milk jugs. The sonogram printout. That September 24, 2020, *New York Times* article by Joshua Sokol, "Why So Blue, Tarantula? A Mystery Gets a New Clue." Wearing scrubs as pajamas. Rebecca Luker, national treasure. Aaron Neville, national treasure. Miss Piggy, national treasure. The purr of a contented cat. David Bowie's recording of "As the World Falls Down." V-neck T-shirts. Beekman 1802 "Rose Apothecary" goat milk soap. A pile of kids' snow boots on a mat next to the back door. Backstage passes. Deciding to do what's needed. Jackie O's giant sunglasses. That 2020 Brian Mashburn painting *Barred Owl*. Moleskine notebooks. A rowboat gliding along on a smooth lake. That first hint of the leaves changing. Soaking the pan overnight. Palmolive. That 1945 Ansel Adams photo *Morning Mist, Merced River and Bridalveil Fall, Yosemite Valley, California*. The Langham Hotel, London. The Dream Inn, Santa Cruz. The Greenbrier, Sulphur Springs, West Virginia. The little tab that helps you unwrap the Hershey's Kiss. The Cure's recording of "Close to Me."

Captain Stubing and Julie and Doc and Isaac and Gopher and Vicki.

Butterfly clips in a variety of sizes.

Sharpies in a variety of colors.

Photos in your pocketbook.

An expert shuffle of the deck of cards.

Happy-making things in a difficult world:

Faded roses. Your preferred Google Alerts. The *Law & Order* between-scenes transitional *dun-dun* sound. Popping the bottle cap with an old-fashioned can opener. Those How to Build a Life columns in *The Atlantic* by Arthur C. Brooks. Satchel Paige, national treasure. Jacques d'Amboise, national treasure. Agnes Moorehead, national treasure. The 2005 revival of *Sweeney Todd* in which all of the actors were the orchestra and played their own musical instruments. **Ants marching in a perfectly straight line.** Dave Matthews Band's recording of "Crash Into Me." Unabashedly showing off the engagement ring. **The ring of a bicycle bell.** Almira Gulch pedaling that bicycle. Martha Stewart's photos on *The Martha Blog.* The fact that in 1880, Queen Victoria gave the Resolute Desk to President Rutherford B. Hayes, and that there were four desks in total made from the remains of the HMS *Resolute.* New Year's resolutions that make it past March 1. *Slightly Foxed* magazine. Recycling as much as you can. **Using what is at hand.** That October/November 2019 *Garden & Gun* story by CJ Lotz, "The Magic of Moss." The fact that Lake Superior is 350 miles long and 160 miles wide. That Hala Alyan poem "Spoiler." The moment after you teach the dog how to "shake" its paw. The Japanese ceremony of Toro Nagashi. Obeying the doctor's orders. Playing devil's advocate. Culture Club's recording of "Time (Clock of the Heart)." Bowler hats.

Happy-making things in a difficult world:

The Stickley Audi Ellis table lamp. Books with bound ribbons as bookmarks, specifically those from the Everyman's Library. Organizing the bills in the cash register drawer. **Power-washing the house.** That Ephraim Pottery *Foretelling Ceramic Pottery Vase.* That moment when you realize the air conditioners are no longer needed. Diana Krall's entire *Live in Paris* album, but specifically her recording of "Just the Way You Are." The Fraunces Tavern Museum. The Jewish Museum. **The Hispanic Society Museum and Library.** The fact that there is a basketball court on the fifth floor of the United States Supreme Court. The fact that in 1937, Abraham Lincoln's granddaughter Mary Lincoln Isham donated the contents of Lincoln's pockets from April 14, 1865, at Ford's Theater to the Library of Congress. That 1924 Georgia O'Keeffe painting *Dark Abstraction.* Perfectly ironed pleats. The spin of the roulette wheel and the click of the roulette ball. **Embracing the struggle.** Loosening the tie at the end of a long day. Seeing a heron take flight. Speed Buggy. Dastardly and Muttley. An ancient wrought-iron daybed covered in an old quilt. Outkast's recording of "Hey Ya!" **Knowing how to replace a zipper.** An implausibility of gnus. An array of hedgehogs. A blessing of narwhals. That May 8, 1968, Robert Knudsen photo *Portrait of Lady Bird Johnson at the White House.* A red-hot water bottle. Reflecting pools.

MIXTAPE: *Time to Make the Doughnuts*

Good morning! The whole day stretches in front of you. Today can be anything you want it to be, and if a curveball comes your way, try to knock it out of the park. Here's a mixtape of twenty songs to start your morning, beginning with a little gem from *Groundhog Day*. Be the hero of your day.

"I Got You Babe" –Sonny & Cher	"Midnight Train to Georgia"
"Manic Monday" –The Bangles	–Gladys Knight and The Pips
"You Are My Sunshine" –Ray Charles	"Jump Around" –House of Pain
"Light of a Clear Blue Morning"	"Every Day Is a Winding Road"
–The Wailin' Jennys	–Sheryl Crow
"Just Call Me Angel of the Morning"	"Life Is Just a Bowl of Cherries"
–Kyla Fletcher	–The Platters
"Good Morning Starshine" –*Hair*	"Let's Go Crazy" –Prince and the
(Original Broadway Cast)	Revolution
"Here Comes Your Man" –Pixies	"Boogie Woogie Bugle Boy"
"Good Morning Baltimore" –*Hairspray*	–Bette Midler
(Original Broadway Cast)	"Rise Up" –Andra Day
"I Am What I Am" –George Hearn	"Birdhouse in Your Soul" –They
"Feeling Good" –Nina Simone	Might Be Giants
"Let's Talk Dirty to the Animals"	"Heroes/Helden" (German album
–Gilda Radner	version) –David Bowie

Happy-making things in a difficult world:

Believing the prophecy of the Magic 8-Ball. HGTV's *Home Town*. Laurel Mercantile's Scotsman Woodshop. Pulling up the rope ladder into the treehouse. **Birds resting on a wire.** A Saturday visit to Rural King. Hall & Oates's recording of "I Can't Go for That (No Can Do)." Mike and Molly and Carl and Victoria and Joyce and Vince and Samuel and Peggy and Jim. That 1963 Andy Warhol painting *Triple Elvis.* **Picking up the birthday cake at the bakery.** Rosettes made of icing. That September 25, 2020, Inspired Life column in the *Washington Post* by Cathy Free, "This Cashier Loaned a Customer $12. A Grateful Community Repaid the Cashier More Than $11,000." Wellfleet. Truro. Hyannis. **Vintage glass cake stands and domes.** Someone who says, "Of course I would do it if I were you." Someone who says, "Of course you can put me down as a reference." Someone who says, "Of course you can call me." Lesley Gore's recording of "It's My Party." Quincy Jones, national treasure. Marin Mazzie, national treasure. Maureen Dowd, national treasure. That 1985 Bruce Weber photo *Ella Fitzgerald, Los Angeles, CA.* A WELCOME HOME! sign. An afternoon wine tasting. **Linus's blanket.** Peppermint Patty and Marcie. **"Sir."**

Happy-making things in a difficult world:
The final lap of the Indy 500. Ellen Raskin's 1978 novel, *The Westing Game.* **The day your child masters tying their shoelaces.** That Annie Leibovitz photo *Queen Elizabeth II, London, March 2007.* An occasion that calls for **a cluster of helium balloons.** Your first time on a skateboard. A head full of pink hot rollers. Level 42's recording of "Something About You." Placing a brand-new Paper Mate Arrowhead Pink Pearl Cap Eraser on the top of a new pencil. Statler and Waldorf. Edina and Patsy. Timon and Pumbaa. That 1869 Edgar Degas painting *The Orchestra at the Opera.* Blueberry pancakes. The moment after the dishwasher is emptied. The moment your eyelids start to get heavy and you know that **it's time for bed.** The moment after the top collar button is unbuttoned. Herman and Lily and Grandpa and Marilyn and Eddie and Spot. Sarah Brightman's recording of "Meadowlark." Looking at your parents' old report cards. **A good gin and tonic.** Dinner with out-of-town friends in their town while on your business trip. An overnight with friends on your way to your vacation destination. Workable exterior shutters. Deniece Williams's recording of "Let's Hear It for the Boy." The fact that a human skeleton is made up of 206 bones. The fact that the Nile River is 4,132 miles long. The fact that it's 238,900 miles from Earth to **the moon.** Lisa Hannigan's recording of "Moon River."

And because it bears repeating:

Lin-Manuel Miranda

(and his iconic gray
"The Sweater").

Things You Might Consider Doing Today

Dye your hair a crazy—and temporary—color. Touch up the paint on the worn spots on the back porch. **Reorganize the sock drawer.** Watch the "Just Christmas, Baby" episode of *black-ish* (season 3, episode 10). Drop off a couple of desserts at the local firehouse. Look at that 2016 Henrietta Harris painting *Fixed It II*. Drive the speed limit. Pick out a new pair of eyeglass frames, even if you don't buy them. Learn how to spell your name in Morse code. **Blast Siouxsie and the Banshees' recording of "Kiss Them for Me."** Move the television out of the bedroom. Make a bet, literally or figuratively. Look at that 1938 Alfred Eisenstaedt photo *Katharine Hepburn, New York City.* Shake out the doormat. Think about what your dream kitchen would look like. Google image search "sunset + Grand Canal Venice." Listen to that 1998 *Fresh Air* interview with Ray Charles, rebroadcast on November 24, 2016. Wash the car. **Eat snacks for dinner.** Listen to Ethel Waters's recording of "A Hundred Years from Today." Subscribe to *People* magazine. Call a relative you haven't spoken to in a while. Bake some chocolate chip cookies. Say thank you for three important things in your life. Plan accordingly.

The Things That Last

The ruins of Pompeii were discovered in 1748. Beethoven's Fifth premiered in 1808. Chicago's Union Station opened in 1925. Gordon Parks's photography career exploded in the 1940s. The Beatles won the Grammy for Best New Artist in 1965. Louise Penny had her first novel published in 2005 at the age of forty-six. These pieces of art, and the artists themselves, have stood the test of time, as have so many of the things you've read about or discovered in this book. But memories, sayings, recipes, and feelings—such as love—can reach a level of immortality as well. There is one final story I'd like to share with you, and it relates to the dedication of this book. Stay with me here; it starts off a little rocky.

My mom's parents died tragically in a car accident in May 1960. My mother, then five years old, and several of her seven siblings were in the car with them and survived. When my maternal great-grandmother learned of her daughter's death, she had a heart attack and died that same day.

Some fifty years later, I visited my grandparents at the cemetery for the first time. I had never been; the memories were too painful for my mom, and we rarely, if ever, talked about her childhood. Yet on that trip home, I wanted to find them. My uncle Dennis, the family genealogist on my dad's side, knew the exact country road that would lead us to the tiny church. We did not, however, know the location of their final resting spot.

That summer day was hot. Record-breaking hot. The heat was oppressive; the humidity felt like an object, something in physical form pressing against every part of your being. That afternoon, in the blistering heat, amid the full-throated song of the cicadas, my uncle and I traipsed the entire cemetery, looking for their graves, but with no luck, finally giving up. Disappointed, we walked back to the car, brown grass crunching beneath our feet, consoling ourselves with the promise of a stop at the Dairy Queen on the way home.

Drenched with sweat, I started the rental car and cranked the AC. The air began to blast, first thermal, then transitioning to a crisp cool, and as I began to shift the car into drive, I took one last look at the churchyard. There, directly to my left out the driver's-side window, literally next to the car, was the gravestone of Walter and Vivian Vaughn.

I said to Dennis as I killed the ignition, "My God, they were right here the whole time. And we were going to leave." I was almost angry with myself for giving up when they were so close. He became very quiet, then opened the door and said, "They were calling out to you." We got out and approached the grave.

It was an oddly surreal and special moment for me.

As I stood at the resting place of my grandparents, I thought about how much my mom has sweated every detail of our lives: ordering yearbooks, attending school and family functions, filling out Scholastic *Weekly Reader* orders, getting up early to start a perfect Thanksgiving dinner, making beautiful scrapbooks, sewing our Halloween costumes, driving to band/dance/poms rehearsals, wrapping a minimum of ten gorgeous presents to rest beneath the Christmas tree, checking homework, celebrating birthdays, confirming brushed teeth, having late-night talks, making sure Easter baskets were waiting for us in the morning, and on and on and on. All this love, shown in small moments, steadily, throughout our entire lives.

Big moments define your life as a child, but only later, when you really are able to think about and process them as an adult, do you realize how easily the small moments are taken for granted, and the value they can add to the rhythm of your being. Because if you lose your parents when you are five, and things are tough, and then they get very tough, you may not have had those touchstones. Or had someone to give them to you. But my sisters and their children and I do, thanks to my mom, who, even though she lost her own parents at five, made sure our lives were full of little pieces of hope.

This makes me believe that Walter and Vivian, and Vivian's mother, Rena White, loved each other fiercely. I choose to further believe that their love was imprinted on my mother (and her siblings), and it silently shaped and buffeted her fundamentally over the years, making its way on to my siblings and me.

Put simply: Love begets further love. Love lasts.

And so, as we finish, I want to remind you: One little piece of hope on a train ride home inspired this entire book into being. One small glance out a window helped me tap into a family legacy of love. The moral of this story? Look out the train window, look out the car window, before you give up and drive away. You never know what you might see—and what inspiration or solace you might find—on the other side of the glass.

Acknowledgments

There are several people who helped make this book a reality and I will be forever in their debt:

Randy Losapio, who takes care of everything and is always there for me.

Agent extraordinaire Brettne Bloom at The Book Group, who is the dream maker and believed in me from my very first Instagram post.

Working with the entire Penguin Life team has been a pleasure and a joy, and I am thrilled to be a member of the family, led by the incredible Meg Leder—remarkable editor, visionary, and North Star—who shepherded this book into being in its entirety. Thank you, Meg, from the bottom of my heart. Josie Portillo, it was an honor to have you join this project—your incredible art inside and beautiful cover outside elevate this book beyond my wildest conjuring. Sabrina Bowers, your vivid imagination and creative designs took my very simple text and made it into A Real Book. Randee Marullo and Karen Wise, your guidance, attention to detail, and expert eyes made everything in the book better. Brianna Harden and Paul Buckley, the cover you created with Josie is so cheery and happy and full of joy—it is electric and alive, and just absolutely perfect. To the wonderful publicity—Rebecca Marsh, Sara DeLozier, and LeBria Casher—and marketing—Molly Fessenden and Amanda Inman—dream teams: a huge thank-you for everything you have done on behalf of the book. Patrick Nolan was a champion from the start, and I am so grateful to you, Madeline McIntosh, and Brian Tart. A special thank-you to the PRH and Penguin sales force—you are the best in the business and incredible colleagues.

I'd also like to thank the following: Kristin Cochrane, who was the first person to tell me I was writing a book and to go for it. Adriana Trigiani, who has always been in my corner and has done so much for me and my family. Helen Ellis is my publishing guardian angel, first reader, and writing whisperer. Suzanne Herz has always believed in me and been in my corner. Alison Rich continually shows me how to live life to the fullest. Jeremy Finley has been my best friend since childhood and told me I was a writer. Jenny Jackson is a genius editor and riddle solver, and now a talented writer in her own right. John and Renee Grisham and Shea and Mike Linden—thank you for cheering the loudest and for your friendship. Margaret Atwood talked up my book at her own events—she is forever The Literary Goddess (TLG). Chris Bohjalian has applauded my efforts from the start, and I'm grateful to him for the moniker "Comforter-in-Chief." Erin Morgenstern read the posts from the beginning and said she knew it would become a book. Ariel Lawhon and Lisa Patton always checked in and treated me like a real author. Richard Pine is a class act and generous soul. Amy Einhorn is the epitome of grace and friendship. Sally Marvin, I wish we could celebrate with a cosmopolitan at Bobby Van's—thanks for always steering me in the right direction. Ruth Liebmann, your support means more to me than you will ever know. Chuck Palahniuk, thank you for your generosity and for being a mentor and friend over the years. Mari Andrew, thank you for your very kind words. Sarah Jenks-Daly, thank you for making my first interview happen and for being a champion of books and authors at large (including this one!).

I would also like to thank my friends and family whom I love very much: Dee and Linda Church; Alison Church and Jackson and Harper Davies; Caitlin, Nathaniel, Logan, and Ava Snoddy; my Papa and Grandma, Jim and Peggy Doughty, who are missed every day; their parents, Andrew and Evelyn Doughty and Ebb and Ginny Curry; Dennis Doughty and Gil Costas; Brad Doughty and Stefanie Simpson; Danny and Patti Doughty; Courtney, Greg, Emy, and Max Poole; Bryce and Lauren Doughty; Earl "Uncle Bob" Doughty; Jean Hanks; my Mimmie and Papaw, Evadean and Robert Church, and my entire Church family; my Granny and Pap, Freeda and Evan Hall; Pam and Johnny Finley; Rebecca, Eve, and Charlotte Finley; Casey Hampton and Jeffry Stanton; Pat and Dick Broadbent; Pat and Eugene Bullard; Sheri Hunter and Connie Church; Dan and Laurel Martin; Nancy Kienzler; Risha Margolis; Parissa and Scott Snider; Jamie Harris; Margot and Mal Eisenberg; Susan Tetterton; Rob Gomes; Melissa Nicholas; Roman Schreiner; Candice Millard; Hampton and Anne Sides; David Grann; Kevin Kwan;

Walter and Vivian Vaughn's children and my mom's siblings, Joyce Rich, Gene Vaughn, Donna Goodrich, James Vaughn, Brenda Faron, Janice Swanson, and Sandra Rich.

Mommo, I wish you could have been here to buy the first copy as we had planned, but I'm glad you knew the book would be dedicated in part to you (and your son). We miss and love "yous." A special shout-out to Lance, Kerry, CJ, and Erika Losapio, as well as the Maryland Three: Nicole Petroski, Amy Graunke, and Dan Losapio. Sending a wave across the pond to Biba, Zbynek, Jakub, and Vojta Machat.

Thank you to all the incredible Doubleday authors and Knopf Doubleday Publishing Group colleagues who have made going to work each day for the past sixteen years an absolute joy. Thank you to all of the amazing booksellers and devoted media contacts and partners who have supported all our books—we literally could not do it without you.

Finally, I would like to extend a very special thank-you to Jeri Krassner and Amy Edelman, who led me to my first job at Random House in the summer of 1998, and to Carol Schneider and Tom Perry, who then opened the door at 201 East Fiftieth Street and gave me my publishing life. Thank you for taking a chance on me all those years ago.

"Bless you, my angel. And pace yourself."

—Cicely Tyson, *The New York Times*, September 26, 2013